REBOUND

The Life Struggles We All Face

LINVAL R. MORRIS

**New Day
Publishing**

Copyright © 2024 REBOUND: The Life Struggles We All Face by Linval R. Morris. All rights reserved.

New Day Publishing
ISBN: 979-8-218-39041-9

This book may not be reproduced, stored in a retrieval system, transmitted, or otherwise copied, in whole or in part, including embedded images, in any form (beyond that copying permitted by Sections 107 and 108 of the U.S. Copyright Law and except by reviewers for the public press), without written permission of the author, except where permitted by law. This permission must be granted beforehand and includes any and all reproductions intended for non-commercial and/or non-profit use.

Cover design by GermanCreative
Photographer / Madison Avenue Photography

Printed in the U.S.A.

Praise for Linval R. Morris

REBOUND
The Life Struggles We All Face

The book is interesting and provides some good information and suggestions for persons who might have experienced or are experiencing challenges on ways in which they might rebound from a negative situation.

Dr. Devon Duhaney, Professor

This self-help book instructs the reader on how to live a more fulfilling, satisfying and happier life as well as reinforces and supports the idea that we all have the ability to change, to make better choices and to become valuable members of our community. He does this by modeling behaviors, repeating words of encouragement, and citing examples of how others have transformed their lives.

Gail Schneider, Education Specialist

The book targets those who have encountered a variety of challenges and are seeking to change their situation for the better.

Contents

Preface
Acknowledgements
Chapter 1 1
Daddy Never Told Me....(no one did) 1
   There Are No Problems Without Solutions 8

   Change the Mindset 10

   Trust Me It Works 12

Chapter 2 21
I Wish I Knew 21
   Living Without Limbs 31

   Baby Steps 35

   All Things Come at a Cost 38

Chapter 3 45
Make That Move (take the shot) 45
   Am I Willing to Change? 48

   How Badly Do I Want to Change? 49

   Will I Seek Help? 50

   (See resources on pages 191-193) 50

   Stand Your Ground and Stay on Course 52

Chapter 4 61
A New Way of Thinking 61
   We Can Accomplish Much Through Determination 63

   Finding Your Inner Strengths and Using Them 65

   Spot Check (How are you doing?) 67

Chapter 5 71
The Way Forward 71
Moving Towards Success and Achieving It 71
   Plan Ahead...Be Willing to Learn 76

   Develop a Belief System 83

   Believe in something bigger than yourself 83

   Adopt a Mentor Strategy 88

   Someone or Something to Look up to 88

Chapter 6 . . . 97
Are We There Yet? . . . 97
Depending on where you want to go... . . . 97
Chapter 7 . . . 111
Stop and Smell the Roses . . . 111
Chapter 8 . . . 125
Lend a Hand . . . 125
Be Continuously Grateful . . . 125
   The Good You Do Will Come Back to You . . . 127

   Five Points of Kindness From a Stranger . . . 130

   He Attended to the Man's Wounds . . . 133

   He Carried the Wounded Man . . . 134

   He Paid For His Care . . . 134

   He Promised Future Payment . . . 135

   The Power of One . . . 138

Chapter 9 . . . 145
Who Do I Want to Be? . . . 145
   Are You Happy With Yourself? . . . 149

   Where Are You Now? . . . 151

   The Diminishers . . . 153

   The Illuminators . . . 155

   The Creators . . . 155

   The Innovators . . . 157

Chapter 10 . . . 161
The Bottom Line . . . 161
Chapter 11 . . . 175
Looking Back . . . 175
Will I Seek Help? . . . 191
Refer to Chapter 3 . . . 191
Resources . . . 192
Resources . . . 193
Mentoring Plan . . . 194
Refer to Chapter 5 . . . 194
Action Plan . . . 197
Action Plan . . . 198
Works Cited . . . 199
About the Author . . . 201

Preface

This book is geared towards anyone who is feeling disappointed in themselves, suffering from lack of self-confidence, feelings of fear, hopelessness, and an unfulfilled Life. I offer simple, practical tips and encouragement about ways in which anyone can help themselves become more productive, positive, and better prepared individuals able to deal with existing or unexpected issues in life. We all want and deserve to experience life at its best. Things may happen to disrupt our lives. Whether it was a result of mistakes we made or not, always remember that there are no problems without solutions. You can bring about change in your life and the lives of others.

Let's get ready to Rebound

Approach to this Book

Before you read this Book, please clear your mind of any of the following:

- Preconceived notions

- Preconceived ideas

- Things you may have been previously taught

- Anything that may have influenced your thinking regarding habit changing

This is extremely important; an open mind will be more accepting of encouragement, suggestions and instructions. Many people have not benefited from good advice simply because they are unwilling to accept change. It is said that if you keep doing something the same way you will get the same results. Don't expect change using the old way that didn't produce the desired result. Think about this just for a moment. Tadpoles can only survive in water because they are unable to be mobile on land. They have to transition to a more advanced state, (becoming frogs), then they are able to take advantage of both land and water. My sincere hope for all who struggle with issues such as, self-worth, dissatisfaction with life, a fear of failure, loss of hope and being unhappy about where they are at this point in their own lives that you will open your mind to follow a new path that will lead you to a place where you can Rebound and be Restored to a Renewed life.

Acknowledgements

I would like to take this opportunity to thank all wonderful people who have been a source of help to me while writing this book.

My deepest thanks, appreciation, and admiration go to Dr. Susan Sosoo, who has been a source of strength and encouragement during this project. Her words of encouragement, moral support, and dedication are notably unmatched in relation to anything, or any project I have ever undertaken. She has worked tirelessly to ensure that every intricate detail was given nothing less than the highest quality of attention. She surprised me one morning during one of daily conversations, by inadvertently mentioning that she was up late the night before and earlier than I would have that morning working on <u>Rebound</u>. Quite honestly, I've not known dedication as was shown by Dr. Sosoo. The quality of her work goes above and beyond. As CEO of Advanced Academics Prep and a well decorated Educator, I expected nothing less; nothing but the best is what she produces. My sincerest thanks and my deepest heartfelt appreciation to Dr. Sosoo.

A million thanks to my little sister Mrs. Annett Prince whose Book Relaunching Ceremony I attended in October, 2023 for unknowingly inspiring me to get with the program and restart my writing. Her five children's books are available on Amazon.

I would like to thank Dr. Veronica McLymont, my big sister, who is the first published author among my siblings. Thank you so much for the example you've set. I'm proud to follow in your footsteps. Her most recent book, Embrace Your Best Self, is available on Amazon.

Thank you to my very close and respected friend, Dr. Devon Duhaney. I felt his excitement and readiness in his response when I asked him to be one of my proofreaders. Thank you for your kind support and willingness to respond so promptly. Thank you my friend.

When I had the idea to write a book, I wondered whether it would become a reality. Should I proceed? As the days and weeks, actually months passed, I found that I was more and more convinced that it had a place in the hands of worthy readers. So, I started writing out of a deep concern for people who I came into contact with quite often because of my past and present jobs, and those who were thankful for the advice and encouragement I gave them.

I am extremely humbled and gratified having seen most of those precious lives evolve into a new way of living and changed into successful lives. They took the advice, ran with it, and Rebounded. I hope all who read it will be inspired to take that first step to achieve change.

Nothing will be achieved if you stay in your comfort zone. You must be willing to venue beyond those boundaries.

Chapter 1
Daddy Never Told Me....(no one did)

The only constant in life is change. We may not be able to control the fact that things are constantly changing, but we can control how we respond to those changes. We can control how we change to live in harmony and with gratitude for the growth change promises. Without change, we would stagnate, and eventually wither. As they say, "Be the change you want to see."

Many of us were not privileged enough to have grown up or be born into a loving or traditional home with both parents who were actively involved in our everyday life and development. While some were fortunate to have both parents present who were somewhat involved and supportive, there were still those missing pieces such as, vital information sharing, practical leadership by example, guidance, and a clear understanding of the changes we experienced while growing up.

Then of course, there is a very large number of us who were unfortunate enough not to have either of the aforementioned luxuries of a sound family life in our early, mid or late developmental stages. An unimaginable number were adopted or abandoned, and many grew up in a single parent household which breeds an enormous legacy of disadvantages, some of which will be highlighted throughout this book. Let's not forget those who survived gross abuses. According to the Pew Research Center, approximately 23% of children under the age of 18 live or grew up in single parent homes (Pew Research Center, 2019). This is quite shocking. I'm not saying that children raised by a single parent can't grow up to be successful, happy and fulfilled. It is just more difficult and they face more obstacles.

The Congressional Coalition on Adoption Institute reports an astonishing 53,500 children have been adopted and we can certainly expect this number to grow (Congressional Coalition on Adoption Institute, 2021). Although the percentage of unplanned pregnancies decreased from 51% in 2008 to 45% in 2011 (National Center for Health Statistics, 2003), the statistics are still high and it is not surprising that there are so many people who are totally unprepared for the difficulties we're bound to encounter in life.

One cannot deny the vast number of missed opportunities for equipping us with the skills needed to prepare us for this adventurous and uncertain journey called life. Pausing just for a moment, how many times have I, you and countless others uttered these words "Daddy never told me.....no one told me...I never knew or thought this could or would happen to me and worst of all, I have no idea what to do or how to handle this." It is true that there may not be a clearly drawn map that will leave us problem free. Without the existence of the perfect playbook, there is the possibility that things could have been very different in our lives. Do not for one moment or at any point misunderstand that I am placing blame on parents, guardians, or whomever was tasked with one's upbringing, on the contrary. The truth goes back to this indisputable fact "life offers no guarantees of a problem free existence; the challenge we're faced with, is how do we deal with the issues as they arise?"

Where am I going with this you may be wondering? I promise you, it becomes clearer as you read on. I also promise you that wherever or in whatever situation you find yourself at any time in your life, you don't have to stay there. There is a way through it and a way out of it. Too often people stay too long at these stop signs or hesitate to proceed because they fail to see a clear path. We often get stuck at the "what ifs." What if things don't work out? What if I do the wrong thing? What if I fail? I hesitate to admit that these questions have their places but I want us to distance ourselves from fear and a negative mind set. The aim is to get you to start thinking about your situation and thinking forward to a plan of action. What will be your next move from where you are to where you want to be? It doesn't matter who you are or what you have achieved. Life certainly can be problematic. We encounter health issues, financial issues, and complicated relational and social issues. We encounter problems at work with the boss, the person in the next cubicle. Although we may not want to admit it, sometimes we are the problem. Not everyone is capable of handling stress. We are unable to compartmentalize. Our frustration gets the better of us which affects our attitude making it more difficult to get along with others. We become angry, angry at the world, angry at God. Now you hate everyone; everyone suddenly turns into the villain and "poor me" ends up as the unfortunate victim. Always look at yourself in the most honest way possible and you might find something you'll need to work on. No one is perfect. We can always be a better version of ourselves.

We are never quite prepared for obstacles and that is why we are thrown into frenzy with little or no control. Our thought pattern changes dramatically, we can't think straight, our heads start spinning, we lose control and for some it seems like the end of the world. For most people, negative thoughts are the first to surface. Negative thoughts produce negative reactions and now it becomes impossible to even consider the slightest chance of a positive outcome. Why do people always say the words "calm down" to an upset individual? To be able to respond sensibly and rationally to any emergency, one has to be in a calm and controlled state of mind. Keep in mind always, that our thought process and pattern determine how we act. Most people react as opposed to respond. Remember the goal is to get you to start thinking differently. There is a choice you must make if you want to bring about change in your own life.

Life does get rather complicated. Most of the difficulties we are confronted with are not in the playbook, and they are in most cases never anticipated. These situations come out of the proverbial "blue" as is often said. They occur unexpectedly at different times and are almost never planned. They are personal, very personal, so then, all things considered, we can agree that it's generally easier to respond to those situations we were briefed on and are now on our own to sort out the unexpected. Now it is up to you to find the answers to these questions. It is now up to you to make the decision to change and then take that first step.

One of the most difficult situations one might face is being born with an extreme birth defect such as, no arms, no legs, or neither arms and or legs. I've known many people who have excelled and are extremely talented despite their disability. Some of these individuals are motivational speakers; many of them are doing everyday chores which would have been considered impossible for someone with such disabilities. I know of one young man with no arms but he is an excellent guitarist....he uses his toes, how amazing is that? Are you getting the idea? Is it becoming clearer? The purpose of this book is for you to open your mind to a sense of possibilities toward finding solutions for the problems that occur in your lives from time to time. There are no solutions, no way out...Absolutely not. Such thoughts are definitely untrue; there is a solution for every problem. I will highlight a number of real life situations as we go along but let's go back to my friend who plays the guitar with his toes. A most incredible accomplishment, take a moment to consider this, and for those of us who play that instrument, isn't it puzzling that someone could master such an instrument with their toes? The question is: Is this a supernatural miracle or is it the result of determination to do something remarkable? How much effort went into doing this? Obviously it required a lot and he succeeded. How many hours of trying? How many days, weeks, months, or maybe even years did it take? I know for a fact that just to get to the stage where one can properly position the fingers to hold a chord, takes quite a lot of effort and trials. If this young man could do this with his toes, consider what you could accomplish with ten fingers. How important was learning to play the guitar to him, I wonder? What inspired him to try? I can only assume it was born out of a deep desire to overcome an unimaginable obstacle.

There Are No Problems Without Solutions

Over two decades ago, I met a man who came to the United States of America from one of the Caribbean islands. He arrived with just a few pieces of clothes in a bag. He had no place to call home; he literally lived on the subway. He found a very low paying job and was able to feed himself, worked during the daytime and slept on the train at nights. Later on, he enrolled in night school while still sleeping on the train. He eventually received his diploma. This allowed him to obtain a much better paying job; he was able to pull himself out of the mess he found himself in. I'm sure this was not how he planned it. Maybe his original plans failed. More likely than not, what happened could have been a case of an unexpected event. Quite possibly a lack of finances may have led to him losing his apartment or home. He obviously didn't want to stay in that situation and so he made a decision to bring about change. He took that first step. Not too many of us would subject ourselves to do what he did. His story was so encouraging to me and many others. Somehow this man used his success story to motivate people he came in contact with, both in everyday life and also through public speaking. In his mind, that was the way out for him. He took the idea and ran with it and found his pot of gold at the end the proverbial rainbow. There's always a solution to every problem... We've heard of many rags to riches stories and amazing achievements born out of desperate situations. While I applaud these results and advancements, this book is not focused primarily on gaining wealth, not wealth as in money but wealth as in a mindset. The goal is to get you to confront your deepest fears, frustrations, feelings of desperation, confusion, weakness, addictions and other conditions and bring change to your life. Nothing is ever as bad as it seems and yet for millions of people it appears to be the end of their world and they crumble and give up when they're faced with difficulties. This mind set has defeated and continues to defeat countless individuals. It ultimately becomes your personal responsibility to effect change.

I will be repetitive; nothing is as bad as it seems and there is a solution to every problem. The questions are, what are you willing to do? How far are you willing to go? And how much effort will you put into seeking the solution? Don't get me wrong or think that for a single moment I'm discounting the severity of any of these issues you and many others are faced with. On the contrary, I'm fully aware and am sympathetic to each case. How you decide to handle it is the challenge. Are you up for the challenge? Actually the challenge is what most people aren't up for because to them it is hard work. Oh how I love technology, and we live in such a technologically advanced world. Everything is immediate. No one wants to wait; patience is a thing of the past and so is hard work. I'm an advocate for working smart and will always encourage that, but to achieve some things, hard work is required without question. When a person gives up on hope for change or fails to allow themselves the benefits of change, life becomes pointless; you are overcome by feelings of weakness which in turn start to affect your physical and mental well-being. It all begins in the mind.

Change the Mindset

The first emotion that we experience when faced with a difficult situation is fear. Fear breeds uncertainty, and uncertainty causes fear. They are intertwined. Fear is very powerful. It can cause a feeling of losing touch with reality as well as causing physical symptoms like panic attacks. So why am I mentioning all this? It is simply to make you aware of this fact and to help you to understand the state of the mind and some of the things that result from fear. To be honest, I don't really think it is at all possible to prevent the onset of fear in all situations, but you can certainly put up a fight, at least to prevent fear from taking hold of you. While fear is a very powerful emotion, it is not all real; it's a smoke screen, an alarm, a false alarm, Fear tells you that something bad is going to happen to you. It says you are going to fail, it will never get better, things will never change, you will lose, it tells you ...you can't do it. I know from experience. I have been confronted, gripped by, and overcome by fear in the past, so much so that it seemed tangible. It literally made me see things that appeared to be so real. I went through most of my youth living with great fear of several different things until I found the truth, the truth that it was and is a big lie. Once I learned that, I was free and liberated. Things started changing, and I started succeeding. Life was different, a whole new world opened. I was a new man, I felt like a real man, a winning man. Among the amazing things I realized is that I wasted so much time and prevented myself from living a more peaceful life. There were so many missed opportunities; so much was lost because I allowed fear to take control of me. NOTHING IS EVER AS BAD AS IT SEEMS. Once I learned how to conquer my fears, I was able to move forward. I confronted each task thinking...what's the worst that could happen? If fear held me back, I tried harder and with a sense of urgency. I took the attitude that...well, I have nothing to lose ...so do it and see and don't stop. If I don't get it on the first try, keep at it until I finally get it. Not everyone, however, might be able to conquer their fears in a strong confrontational manner. Don't worry! You can take baby steps. It may take several attempts but remember, keep working at it.

Trust Me It Works

Changing your mindset...don't ever let anyone tell you that you can't, don't allow yourself to tell you that you're incapable, that it's too far out of your reach. Be careful who you talk to; be very careful with whom you surround yourself, with whom you hang out, who you listen to and most of all who you follow. It is said that "misery loves company" and failure along with under achievers are no different. Look at your garden or your lawn and notice how fast the weeds grow, how they are able to thrive in almost any condition, how they keep on coming back unless you go to extreme measures to prevent them. Be careful of influencers; take time to think for yourself, and not be too dependent on advice, especially from those who aren't able to handle their own issues but are quick to offer advice. If they are not able to properly advise themselves, what makes them qualified to give advice. Think about it...does that make sense? Daddy may not have told me, no one ever told me when I was growing up but it is not the end. Learning has no age limit, Don't be ashamed to fumble the ball. Life is not the Super Bowl; don't beat yourself up if you are blocked at the hoop. Grab the ball when you can and try again. Keep going at it until you learn how to hold that ball tightly enough so you do not lose it. Keep trying, and keep those eyes open so you can see your opponent coming to block you.

Be very aware of your surroundings. Be extremely conscious of what and who is around you, and know what you're up against and what is against you. I'm not a botanist but from practical experience and observation I found that some plants do not and cannot survive or thrive in certain environments because they need specific nutrients and climatic conditions to survive and thrive. The same is true in life; you may need to physically change your environment to rid yourself of the bad elements that are systemic. Then there are the psychological environmental conditions, which can be very unhealthy for your past and present state of mind. These will most definitely affect your state of being and are guaranteed to keep you oppressed. I mentioned influences earlier and I'm referring to bad influences. There are those who seem to enjoy trampling on others when they're down, taking unfair advantage of your weakness or demise. Just as it is in the business world where corporate takeover is a common practice, many larger, stronger companies have monopolized in this fashion. They specialize in such practices and that is how they become so powerful. No one can say this is wrong because that's how the business world operates. So weak, struggling and failing businesses are prime targets. There may be people in your environment who are like that, so be very cautious and aware. Safeguard against such possibilities, and be on the lookout.

Do not be afraid to self-examine on a regular basis asking yourself questions like: What did I not do that I should have done? What did I do that I shouldn't have? What do I need to know so that the mistakes I made won't be repeated? How do I know when I'm doing the wrong thing or better yet, the right thing…so I get it and I hear you loud and clear? Yes. It was not your fault. Your current situation did not come about because of anything you did, I really do get that but that does not mean that you sit there and mope or sulk, cry, or be angry. At whom? At what? Anger breeds misguided passion; misguided passion makes you do misguided things. It influences your decisions. For a moment, examine yourself. How many times can you honestly say you've done some really foolish things, made some stupid decisions, made some uninformed decisions that you may regret for the rest of your life. We all have been there no matter how simple, those things done out of anger may have been.

So can we fix those blunders? Yes, there may be that possibility but let's try a different approach. Let's make a conscious decision to be aware of the destructive force of anger. Decide to subdue your anger when it comes. After all, who is in control? Is it you or is there something else controlling you? It is your life, the only one you have, the only one you will ever have. How do you want to live it? Who makes that decision? Daddy or Mommy can't make it for you. They are not living in your skin. Sure they can and may be able to help but the ultimate effort is yours to make. Once again there is no rule book; there are no playbooks to outline it all for you. Here is your big moment to shine, your moment to say with pride and gratification.... I DID IT, I FOUND A WAY and I DID IT.

My aim is to get you to think about what lies within you that is dormant. Maybe because of the trauma you've experienced, you believe your inner strengths, abilities and potential have faded or are dead. In reality, with no offence to anyone..... "It's not over, till the Fat Lady sings" ; it's not over until you're dead. But that's not what we really want, is it? We want to live and live well. We don't want to just survive. We want to live our best life. That's why we worry about it so much, why we are driven to depression and frustration and want to give up or entertain the thought that things may never change. We're afraid to face reality. They say that wasting the mind is a terrible thing and it is very true. That is where it all happens, in the mind. Your thoughts can either make or break you; how you think determines how you live. Your thought pattern and process define and ultimately shape you as an individual. You have a responsibility to yourself to control your mind. Anything can be achieved if you put your mind to it. Listen if you don't believe me, try something simple like learning to do something you've always wanted to do but think you can't because you don't know how to, or you "think" you really can't. Stop reading this book right now and try it. Then come back and continue reading and watch your life change before your very eyes. If the mind can conceive it, then the possibilities are endless. YOU CAN DO IT...I know you can. Say it to yourself...YES I CAN.

I can't help thinking of the guy who was born with no arms and legs. He lives a complete and fulfilled life. He has accomplished so much in spite of his disability. This man's life has inspired millions around the world. I'm still learning to play the guitar at my age, yet there is a young man with no arms who plays incredibly well with his toes. There are many stories about people who have pulled themselves out of the clutches of desperation after waking up to the reality that life doesn't need to be a defeated and desperate experience. Many of us have lived for too long with self-inflicted psychological and emotional wounds that continue to haunt them. My friends, it doesn't make a difference how it all started; you have the ability and power to put an end to this suffering. Stop short changing yourself; you don't have to settle.

Personal Notes:

Personal Notes:

Personal Notes:

Chapter 2
I Wish I Knew

I'm lost and confused because I haven't the slightest idea how to handle my issues. High school didn't do much to prepare me. I thought after college I'd be ok, smooth sailing. I've got the world on a string. I've got the string wrapped around my finger, I'm on my way...nothing can stop me now. Isn't that how we think? And yes I agree; that's how we want it to be but unfortunately life is never smooth sailing, no bed of roses. We're constantly struggling with something no matter how small or simple. We're constantly fighting, competing, going against the grain. From birth, life becomes an uphill battle. Think about it. There's always something to manage and it's not, in most cases, always easy. Of course not all of the issues are of a destructive nature but in many cases they certainly are. These are what we should be very mindful of because simple things can develop into complicated things. A large number of people will readily seek professional help such as talking to a psychiatrist, a therapist or a trusted friend, a minister or family member. I fully endorse such efforts wholeheartedly and encourage anyone to seek help. That is a most important thing that is always ignored. No matter how good the advice is, if the person in question doesn't do anything with it, they certainly wasted all the time and money spent on those sessions. When you really think about it, if you the individual only listen to what you are told but do not act, it will not make any difference and there will be no change.

Let's look at the story of a young man who turned his situation around by changing his attitude and his way of thinking. Just because things did not go the way he had hoped, and all looked hopeless for quite a while did not mean that things would not work out to his benefit. Jason graduated from college with honors and was employed as a junior executive at a business management company. Obviously, he was quite a brilliant young man who was brought up in a conventional family setting. He was focused on his career and was on his way. He had the world on a string with hopes of advancement and dreams of having a family of his own before he turned thirty. With that in mind, he felt it was time to start dating. Jason was like his dad who was a dedicated family man. He loved his family and believed deeply in being monogamous and so was Jason. After going on a few not so successful dates and not being like most of the alpha males he worked with, who believed in exploring with the opposite sex and freeform dating, Jason had a hard time making a significant romantic connection. This went on for about a year and a half, and frustration started to set in and it bothered him. That was when he began to question himself, kind of like second guessing whether something was wrong with him. Why does it seem so easy for the other guys to get just about any girl they wanted? It appeared that these guys were literally being chased by women. They were even approached and asked out on dares by these attractive, sexy, beautiful females, but not Jason.

He was just a nice guy, a good guy; everybody liked Jason. The more he tried to control his frustration the more it got the better of him. He was able to hide his feelings when he was with his peers, family and the very few friends he had. Life was becoming somewhat of a drag, the old routine day after day. He had almost lost his self-confidence and it was rather amazing he was someone who appeared to have had it together. It would be astonishing for anyone to know what was happening on the inside. Life was so much different for the other guys who didn't have those immediate goals as Jason did; and one would question if something is wrong. Are his standards unreasonable? What could be the cause of this peculiar situation? Gradually Jason became less sociable, edgy and annoyed. This was becoming noticeable. People recognized the change in his demeanor and even his work habits. He realized however that he needed to exercise better control of what was happening. He was aware that to allow this to get out of hand would be quite destructive. The problem now was how to handle it, what to do about it. He had always wanted his life to be normal, like his dad's, like other men who had a "normal" family life, a good job, a wife and children, buy a home, a family car, go camping, vacations, you know the normal stuff that the average family does. At twenty eight years old his life seemed worthless, pointless. The good thing was that Jason knew and was determined not to let this problem get the better of him.

Daddy never told him, no one told him this would be happening to him, a model citizen, an up-and-coming executive, Mr. nice guy, the one who seemed to have it together. This was a totally unexpected ordeal. May I pause to say again "life offers no guarantees and our plans for our lives may not always go according to how we planned them and may not meet our expectations." Disappointments cause us to stumble, being thrown off track; facing road blocks and delays can make or break us. Situations such as these are a true test to reveal what we are made of, what is inside of us, and who we truly are. We can choose to overcome them or we can lie down.

To some people this might not appear to be that serious of an issue. Some wouldn't allow this to get the better of them. Some of us are stronger and more capable. It may also not be of great importance in terms of a life's goal. Among the many problems we will face, one will get to each of us at some point in our life. Let's however be aware that this is not so much about preparedness as it is about facing it head on when it comes our way and making a conscious decision to beat all the odds stacked against us. In Jason's case, he had the right attitude and he endeavored to keep his head and focus on maintaining his composure. Shattered dreams are never pleasant to experience and as was said before, they can make or break anyone. Realizing the dangers of giving in, he thought that instead of allowing frustration to take control, he would refocus on his career path and stay positive. It was not an easy task but with enough effort and determination he made significant progress. For the most part, he was almost back to normal as he continued to work on himself.

It was a crisp spring afternoon and after work that evening Jason decided to take a walk in the small park not too far from his office building just to relax and watch the older kids play baseball. Amazing how beneficial taking a break from your frustrations can be. He realized after a few minutes that he was actually enjoying watching the game. He was particularly touched by the passion and intensity with which these youngsters were playing. It was obvious how much fun they were having. At the same time, they were all focused on the end goal...winning. Inadvertently he turned around to find a spot where he could be closer and get a better look. To his surprise he bumped into and heard someone say "oh, I'm so sorry." He felt something tight in his chest, and this of course startled him. When he looked up, to his surprise with eyes wide open, he saw what he thought was the most beautiful young woman he'd ever laid eyes on. Struggling for words he muttered...ex....excuse me miss, I'm so very sorry about this...this was my fault...and your dress got messed up. He said again, "I'm so very sorry." She stepped back a bit and smiled at him and said, "oh no it was my fault." Instead of looking where I was going. I was staring at the last play. Wasn't that a great catch? "Oh yeah, it really was", Jason responded. I...I decided to move to a much better spot and that was when I...we bumped into each other. By this time, they were feeling much more comfortable with each other and were smiling delightfully with a kind of awe. A strange but somewhat calming sensation overcame him and from the way she was looking at him he could tell the same was happening to her. They stared at each other with glowing eyes.

This went on for quite a few minutes with a flurry of emotions they could not quite make sense of, just smiling, looking at each other then turning away for just a brief moment repeatedly. "I was just about to go over there", he said, pointing to an opening between the scanty group of spectators close to first base. I think it's better, don't you....? Would you.... Would you like to go with me...that's only if you're not with someone and it's ok with you? Well I'd like to but I'm with a friend from work ...a girl ....we're kind of best friends at work and since it was a nice evening we decided to go for walk here... and...well.. She has a 5:45 date. It's almost...ok, I'll...maybe I will but it all depends on when her date gets here. Let's see what happens... Ok I'll go back and wait with her till she leaves, then I'll join you. If you're still there. Oh you bet...I will be there...I won't move a muscle. Ok she said smiling at him and walked off, turning back just after about twenty five feet. She noticed that he was standing in the same position looking at her. He looked lost but…cute. She smiled at him ever so gently and waved just a little. Jason tried to smile but he was quite a bit in dreamland. He was only able to remove his hand from his pocket just above his waist and waved back. A million and one thoughts were racing through his mind. All the possible scenarios were popping up. First the negative ones, then the positive ones. He literally had lost interest in the game, hoping that she showed up or if she didn't, maybe he would go over. But he didn't want to scare her away or appear too desperate. After all, it had been about a year and three months since he had been on anything close to a real date and of course he would have given an arm and a leg to make this mature into something worthwhile. It was 5.58 pm when he looked at the time on his phone and as he was putting it back in his pocket he heard someone say, "hi...I'm back." He almost passed out, being overcome by surprise and excitement. "So what would you like to do?", he muttered trying hard not to sound as nervous as he felt. "Anything you'd like", she replied. "Oh, forgive me; we haven't been introduced. I'm Jason", he said while extending his hand. "I'm Jen", she responded, extending her hand. Both hands met in the middle and lingered for quite a few moments. They agreed to stop at a nearby coffee shop and while walking; there were more smiles and quick glances at each other, than the number of words they exchanged. To Jason, it was like a whole new world had opened up as they talked with each other with more ease as the evening seemed to pass by so quickly. He could tell she was having a good time also. Amazingly enough, they got along quite well and were obviously enjoying each other's company. When it was time to go, he asked if she was interested in meeting again and she said yes. He offered to walk her to a bus stop and waited there with her until the bus came.

Jason had never in his life felt so confident about anything. For some strange reason, he had a strong sense that things were going to work out with Jen. After dating for approximately one month, they made a commitment to each other. This experience helped him to rebound to his previous state of being. His self-confidence returned, he regained his enthusiasm, he was winning once again. Life was good and everyone around him noticed and commented on the dramatic change in the man who had almost lost himself in despair. About a year later, Jason and Jen got married, and shortly thereafter his first child was born. Jason's life had rebounded; his hopes and dreams were now reality.

For those of you who continue to struggle and live in defeat and despair, know for a fact that all things are possible, whether by faith, patience and perseverance or by continually working on yourself. It is bound to happen. Just don't be derailed by negative thoughts. Change the mindset, remember that you have a responsibility to yourself to always stay positive or a least try your best to get in that frame of mind. Only when you are mentally and emotionally well, can you start taking steps toward a change in your thinking that Will jumpstart your actions toward success.

In Chapter one, I brought up the subject of people who were born with genetic defects and how many of these individuals were able to beat the so called impossible odds stacked against them. Prior to reading a number of their stories the main question that lingered in my mind was, what is the driving force behind their success? What fueled the fire that burned inside them to make them want to beat the odds and propel themselves to a life of contentment and satisfaction? I used to ask myself how anyone can be contented living with overwhelming disadvantages. This intrigued me, and to a point was somewhat disturbing. That was when I decided to take a real in-depth look at it.

Living Without Limbs

In my research, I came across a video on YouTube about a young man who was born without limbs. He was adopted by a family who raised him and today, he has made them extremely proud. The most striking thing to me about his story, in his own words, is that he was not content to be restricted by his disability. He was determined not to be a victim of his circumstance. He wasn't going to be defeated, depressed, or live in despair. Having no limbs means that there will be many things one would not be able to do, many simple things that we take for granted because we are blessed with fully functioning limbs. Think about it for just a moment; imagine your present circumstances, the ones that have you curled up on the couch, rolled up into a ball, feeling sorry for yourself, thinking that your life has no meaning. You're trapped, imprisoned, angry at God, angry at the world, crying, saying... Daddy never told me... no one told me that this would happen to me. I don't know how to handle this; I don't know what to do. The only difference with you and this young man without limbs is that he made a decision to change his situation. He got up and did something positive. He taught himself to walk on what he had; he used his upper body in sync with the lower part and crawled up the stairs. He taught himself to move safely down the same stairs; he used his mouth to hold a pencil and taught himself to write; he attended school which was a huge challenge. He made up his mind to be self-sufficient and show others that he can do most things they can do. This young man joined the dance class; wait a minute how does anyone dance without legs? He learned to dance just like the others and became a very important part of the dance group, performing at all major events held at the school and elsewhere.

Among his many accomplishments, or I should say, the most amazing of his accomplishments, is that this young man did a lot of public speaking, motivational speaking. Incredible, isn't it? He will tell you that it wasn't easy; he had his down days, his so called impossible days. In his own words, "when the negative thoughts come in my head, I tell my myself, I'm going to fight harder, I'm going to push harder and I'm not going to give up until I learn how to do what I set out to do. The things that seem the hardest are what I work on the hardest." His goals were realized, his dreams became reality, he made up his mind not to be dependent on anyone to do for him what he can do for himself. Like I said before, absolutely nothing is impossible to achieve if you put your mind to it. I've known of people who decided to do something about their situation and I really believe they wanted to but never did anything. They just sat there and dream. Does that sound familiar? Have you been there or are you there? How long have you struggled with ....when to start, how to start, or ...I don't have what it takes? I encourage you to put your thoughts into action; don't keep putting it off. Like the slogan says, "just do it." Your life will never change if you don't. There is always a starting point regardless of what the circumstance calls for. If you are afraid, don't sit and wait for the fear to go away because it won't. If you feel weak and powerless, don't wait to feel strong and powerful. If you think that you can't do it because you lack confidence, think of all the people who have accomplished things that others thought were impossible.

Earlier we talked about the brutality of fear and what it can do to you or anyone for that matter. We touched on how fear can make you see, feel and hear things which aren't real. This can be and is a big red stop sign for many, the weakness that is felt, the lack or loss of confidence. This paralyzing emotion has been the downfall of many, but not only has it been the downfall. It has also been a major reason why individuals have not stepped up and made a change in their lives to better themselves. It doesn't just stop there either because for every life that is transformed, it affects the lives of others and those additional positively affected lives affect society and result in the world becoming a better place. The world does not make itself good or bad; the world doesn't make itself better or worse. We are the makers of a better world; we are the ones responsible for transforming world.

Did you know that things are only hard to do when you lack the confidence to delve into the unknown. I always thought that a brake job on any of the cars I've owned was extremely hard to do. I had no experience in doing such a thing and of course that made me think.... Oh no I can't do that. What if I break something or hurt myself? What if I just totally make a mess? Now, after several failed attempts, I do my own brakes. I was able to overcome that fear and prove to myself that I could do it. I can certainly tell you that in the beginning it was not an easy thing. Yes I hurt myself and broke quite a few things but in the process I started hurting myself less and less and broke fewer things. Now I hardly ever break anything and hurt myself infrequently. What's the point of my brake job story? Because I wanted to learn and become proficient in replacing the brakes on my cars, I was willing to risk the things I was afraid of, to accomplish the things that built my confidence. The more I did it, the better I became at it, and that led me to take on many other tasks which were more complicated. No one will be good at everything they set out to do but when it comes down to those things which are vital to living a fulfilling life, it requires you to go the extra mile and be proactive and persistent.

Baby Steps

They say, "Practice makes perfect". An aspiring pianist was on his way to Carnegie Hall in New York City to observe an audition. Somehow he lost his way (these were the days before GPS). After going around in circles for a while, he saw an old man on the corner playing a Violin, you know...one of those street musicians. He stopped and asked..."Sir, how do I get to Carnegie Hall?" The old man barely paid any attention to him, then in a soft but kind of a high pitched voice he said "practice, practice, practice, is the only way you can get there." The young man was quite puzzled and for a moment he stood there pondering what he'd just heard. The old man looked at him and kept repeating the words, "practice, practice, practice." The young man happened to raise his head and there was the sign pointing to his left. He was just across the street from his destination. While sitting in the lobby of this magnificent structure waiting for the amateur performances to begin, he suddenly laughed out loud and clapped his hands. Suddenly it all made perfect sense. An aspiring musician's only hope of becoming proficient at playing his instrument must practice, practice, practice...he had his mind set on one day being a performer on the stage of this world famous venue. The more something is done, the easier it becomes, the better you get at doing it, so don't stop at your first failed attempt at anything you try to do. The young man without limbs did not stop when he rolled down the stairs many times trying to get to the top. He had nothing to lose, no arms or legs to break. It took time, effort and determination. Talk about pain, yes pain. Now, he hobbles up those stairs with ease.

At times we are closer to our destination than we think. At times we're closer to achieving our goals, closer to our turning point, that breakthrough, closer than we realize. Once you start, don't stop, and don't give up. Have you any idea of what a difficult and costly process it is drilling for oil or well water? It involves hundreds of hours, lots of expensive heavy equipment. A lot of broken drills and pumps, personal injuries and sometimes fatalities but they keep on drilling and drilling until that first bit of oil comes spewing up. I've seen grown men deliberately stand there and get soaked in raw crude oil. Why I ask myself? Why do they do it? It's a celebration of winning the prize especially after all it took to get to that place of success.

I'm always amazed watching babies taking their first step, after countless attempts to first stand up on their own and falling down many times. Some have hurt themselves in the process. Have you noticed how determined they are? I've seen them at times get so frustrated that they cry and cry but I also noticed that they never just sit back down and stay still. They kept trying and of course, that first step was never made in most cases on the first day. You can be sure they'll be at it again the next day and the days leading up to when it finally happens. Practice, practice, practice. Remember my friend, once you start, don't stop, even if it's a little bit at a time. Whatever it may be that you want to accomplish, stick with that first step, then a second and a third and keep going at your own pace. We're all different in some ways although still very similar in other ways and abilities. The principles are the same. Get up from where you are, get out there and do it, if necessary again and again. You will succeed.

All Things Come at a Cost

The cost of success will come in different forms and at varying degrees; it's almost never the same for everyone. As I said earlier, you won't necessarily find written rules on how to handle every situation. We are individuals with different skill sets and abilities which will make our approach somewhat unique. It is much difficult for those who did nothing for a long period because of fear, weakness and the lack of the will to take action.

The will and determination to take that first step is of paramount importance. One must be willing to give up something, or somethings. For instance, if a person is overweight, it will require discipline to achieve shedding the number of pounds needed to reach their goal. They will need to change the way they eat and what they eat. Giving up the foods we love and what we're used to eating is a very difficult thing to do. You just don't stop the moment you make the decision to change your eating habits. You now have to battle the cravings and temptation. Imagine walking through the food court at the mall, the very place you have been to almost every weekend. You smell the aroma of those hot delicious Cinnamon Buns. You look around and there's someone biting into one and you notice the facial expressions. You can tell how delicious it really is because for several years you have done the same. Then there are those cheesy fries, French fries, onion rings, the cheese burgers. Oh my, what about fried chicken, and oversized sodas. Those are the things you have consumed over the years which contributed to the weight problem you are now faced with.

Maybe you were told by your doctor that you have no choice but to lose some weight and keep it off. Maybe you find that you have some difficulty undertaking some tasks. It could also be that you want to be able to wear certain types of clothes. The fact is, if you want to lose the weight, you will need discipline. We all are fully aware that exercise is another way of getting rid of extra weight. Now you'll have to get into some kind of routine. We are again confronted with other challenges such as, conditioning the mind to get up and go walking, running, acquiring some exercise equipment or going to the gym. Funny, but I know people, some are close to me, who have quite a few pieces of exercise equipment tucked away in some corner or under the bed and some are even out in the open. The thing they all have in common, is that they haven't been used and in some cases, never been used. Apart from bariatric surgery, liposuction and a few other medical procedures, diet and exercise are the only two other options. Let me be clear, however, I am in no way referring to these other options in a negative manner. Think of all the health benefits of diet and exercise which do not necessarily accompany those other options. A proper diet will lessen some common health risks and prevent some others; it affects your entire body and your mental state in many positive ways. What you consume can either preserve your well-being or cause you to deteriorate.

So let's talk for a little while about some of the costs to achieve your desired weight. You'll have to fight your cravings... Listen, I hear you loud and clear, this I understand fully, and I know what it feels like to have to resist that warm tasty Cinnamon Bun. You smell it, the aroma sinks deep, you try not to look over towards the kiosk, and you feel envy for the guy who is biting into one. You're about to lose control. You start shaking and a million reasons why you should stop and get one clouds your mind. At that moment nothing seems rational because that craving is so strong, so overwhelming.... Congrats, you passed by and didn't look, you didn't get mad at the guy standing right there enjoying his bun. You breathe a sigh of relief. Great job; you did well. That doesn't mean you're out of the woods yet because you still want it, which was the first day of battle. The same goes for all the other tasty fattening foods that have been in your diet for years. It requires discipline to face the upcoming days and weeks and months before you can pass these food items by without a severe struggle. Some people weren't as successful on their first day. George walked by the kiosk with the intention not to even look. As a matter of fact, he walked on the other side to avoid it as much as possible and he really needed to buy some underwear and there was a sale going on at a store not too far from Cinabun World.

He stood in what seemed like the longest line he'd ever been in after finding the Power Rangers underwear he wanted so badly. The wait was torture. The aroma from Cinabun World had permeated the entire mall. He was worn down to the point where after paying for his item, he ended up in another line to get his lifesaving Cinabun. In fact he bought two, no actually he felt he owed it to himself and bought four. His genius plan was to have one then and bring the rest home for his girlfriend, hoping she would appreciate his thoughtfulness and allow him to have one, presumably only one. The sad thing is that the remaining three didn't make it home. "Ok George... It's not the end of the world...you can always try again but until then go easy on the guilt trip." After several weeks of torture, trials and failures, fortunately our good friend George was able to reluctantly detach himself from the cravings because of a warning from his doctor.

Changing habits is never an easy task. It involves so much effort, self-denial, struggle, and discipline. It can make you feel uncomfortably restricted. It's costing you the freedom to have it your way, the right to make your own choices. Some of us go through terrible withdrawal symptoms which lead to frustration and even depression but in the end it is totally worth it, I promise you. Always focus on the end result; focus on the prize, the rewards and the benefits. I proved it personally, without any direction from a medical professional. I wanted to be a certain size for personal reasons and I made that decision. It wasn't easy but I went from a 36 inch waist to a 30 in a matter of months. I also watched my son go from 36 plus to 32, all because we made that decision and stuck to the plan. You can do it, even by baby steps. Honestly my friend I say all this with deep empathy and concern because I am aware of the suffering and anxiety that we all experience at some point in our lives. For a healthy and robust lifestyle I find that diet and exercise go together. They offer similar benefits and are very important to our mental health.

Personal Notes:

Personal Notes:

Chapter 3
Make That Move (take the shot)

Now that you're a bit more aware of the possibility of how things can happen to upset your plans for your life, and you understand the dynamics of the journey of life, the uncertainties and the lack of guarantee, let's get ready for the next move, your move.

I want to speak more directly to those of you who feel weak and helpless simply because you are the ones who need the most help. For anyone who is feeling weak and helpless, the most difficult thing to do is to believe that there is a better way to live and to hope for change. You're now aware that changing your mindset is the beginning of your action plan. Being trapped and bound like that has ruined your self-worth. Now, you have totally given up. If you find that this describes your situation, take a moment to examine yourself honestly.

Ask yourself a few questions:

1. Am I contented being where I am? ___yes ____no

2. Do I want change? ___yes ____no

3. Am I willing to make a change? ___yes ____no

4. How badly do I want to change? ___yes ____no

5. Will I seek help? ___yes ___no

If your answer is yes to all, then we're ready to go, so let's read on. If your answer is no to some or all, I would suggest that you carefully rethink your situation.

Am I content being where I am?....The answer to this question for most people would be "No" but interestingly enough, even though most people really feel that way about wanting change, they find it difficult to make a move towards change. Why is that? Could it be that they have lost the will to at least try? Throughout the years, I've traveled internationally and noticed one thing that remains common wherever I've been. There are people all over the world who struggle with some of the same issues, this says, we're human and vulnerable to so many things. I am not a mental health expert, but it is obvious that there are many people who are experiencing mental health issues.

To these unfortunate ones, I strongly recommend that they seek professional help since recovery processes have advanced dramatically, especially in recent years. It is unfortunate that some were born with such a condition, while others may have developed it due to several verified reasons, which I'm not qualified to address. There are many social and community based programs and organizations that offer help to those in need. Once again, I strongly encourage them to seek help. Having had close interaction with a vast number of individuals who are going through extremely difficult times and trying to pull themselves out of whatever the situation they find themselves in, let take a closer look at the above questions.

This is now all about you. I will not hold anyone's hand; you're going to have to do some work. So you're hurting from whatever your issue is; choose from among those mentioned earlier in the book, and find your category. With an open mind, you have already examined yourself. You know where you are. You know what you want, and you are ready to go after it. Can you see the change you want from start to finish? Not just half way but all the way because the goal is to get out of the mess you're in. You will have to maintain that focus, not to say that there won't be times when you don't feel as strong as you are now. You must keep that focus. Keep your eyes on the Prize!

Am I Willing to Change?

Start thinking differently than you did yesterday. The

days prior to this new day have now become your past, the days of the old you. You are reading this book. That is encouraging. Now you have to see yourself differently. No longer are you weak and helpless, because now you are a living breathing person with all your faculties fully functional and ready for action. All your ambitions are now possible to realize.

How Badly Do I Want to Change?

Find the strength that lives inside you. You owned it before. Somehow it seems that it was stolen from you or maybe you gave it up. I believe that inner strength never leaves a person. It just goes dormant and can be awakened at any time; it just needs to be stimulated. From today, going forward, all that others may have said about you does not currently define you. When you show up at work or in public the next time and someone says, "hey, how's it going?" They should be shocked to hear something other than "oh same sh..t, different day" because your old way of thinking has changed, and you have changed.

Once you get to the place where you know what you want and you're willing to do something about it, your motivation should come from how badly, how much and how urgently you want to see that change come alive. The evolution has begun. Be on your guard to face the stumbling blocks in the way. Don't get side tracked. Be careful not to start doubting yourself. If you fumble the ball and fall, get up and keep going. You'll regain control and then move on to the finish line and if you get knocked down again, get up and repeat the action. Don't give up and don't give in. Be sure that in the end you will win.

Will I Seek Help?
(See resources on pages 191-193)

If for any reason you feel the need for help, by all means ask. There is no shame in admitting to yourself and to others that you need help. Just be careful who you ask. Seek people who can and will help. Talk to those you know who are capable and will have your interest at heart. Make sure the ones you consult are persons who have their lives together and are able to offer sound advice. This may include therapists, doctors, your spiritual leader, a family member or a trusted friend. You're on your way, on the move, on a lifesaving mission. Don't forget to be consistent, Give the television a break, read a good book, and get involved in some activity or activities. Start a new hobby, learn to do something you've always wanted to do or have never done. The idea is to keep you occupied with something worthwhile. Start exercising, run, walk, lift weights, go mountain climbing, cycling, keep your mind and body active. Change your diet, start eating healthy or healthier. Become less dependent on stimulants; feed your mind with good thoughts. Be thankful for having your limbs. Take tips from those who have been where you are and are now living meaningful lives.

Wake up every day with a determination to beat the odds. Find something to laugh about, give yourself a pat on the back for each obstacle you clear. Give yourself enough credit for each thing you do right. Be careful to stay away from negative people with nothing constructive to say. This can be very destructive to your growth and advancement. All these encouraging suggestions are quite simple and may sound like worn out clichés but they are extremely valuable. Be open-minded and see the value. Then it will make sense to you. As you practice these helpful suggestions, you will see things begin to change and you most definitely will start feeling good about yourself.

Catalogue your plan of action, just don't wing it; you need to have something tangible to work with. Track you progress and keep a journal. Set achievable goals, write them down and work towards them but try not to be hasty. It's very likely when doing anything in an impatient manner that you will create a mess and find that you become frustrated. If however that should happen, stop and regroup your thoughts and re think your plans.

Stand Your Ground and Stay on Course

At this point, you have accomplished much and I congratulate you on achieving such a milestone on the journey of self-renewal. You have acknowledged where you are at this stage of your life and condition with which you're not happy. You've acknowledged that you want change, you're willing to change, you want it badly, and you're willing to seek help. Great Job, now the journey begins.

Looking across the broad spectrum, with any task that is of value and is to be completed, it's a certainty that there are going to be issues at some point in the process. Also it's not uncommon in many cases that delays and setbacks do happen. Let's talk a bit about any type of construction project; it is never a seamless flow. I have a friend who is a project manager for a very large construction company. She says, whenever there is a problem free day everyone gets quite nervous. These so called problem free days are very seldom because setbacks and interruptions are extremely frequent; the nature of the industry. Things do happen unexpectedly. There always is a schedule to keep, deadlines to be met, permits to be had, material to be delivered, engineering and reports, different types of skilled workers to be scheduled, depending on the stage of the process. Quite a lot of complicated moving parts, right? What happens when permits are not received on time, the engineers report is not favorable, equipment is not on site, material does not arrive on time, work scheduling upsets, the weather, and a myriad of unforeseen problems and challenges.

So you're trying to sort out your life and I'm here talking about construction problems. Hold on a moment; be patient. There's an important lesson to be learned here. We walk down the street and see heavy equipment clearing an empty lot or demolition going on. There may or may not be a posted sign saying "Coming Soon", so we wonder what's going on. Then later on we notice fences going up and maybe for a period of time nothing happens. Then over the next several months the noise of construction can be heard. Without realizing all the planning and sweating going into this project, as time passed, you then see this beautiful structure and you go, "wow," that's really nice.

Be aware that the process of life is not much different from the process of constructing a building. So much is required to build a proper foundation for an individual's life, that is if that individual wants to have a good life. For example a person who is able to retire earlier than most had to set up a very good and profitable life savings and investment portfolio. Unless there was some form of inheritance or financial windfall, the only other practical way would have been as I mentioned before, a saving and investment portfolio. In any case, proper planning would have to be done. This would require sufficient time and an adequate amount of money being put away.

Rebuilding your life will most definitely encounter some setbacks, disappointments, discouragements and some hitches. Don't be thrown off track; stand your ground and stay on course. Just as the construction project was able to be completed after working out the kinks and the disruptions, they kept on going because there was a structure to be completed, maybe later than was scheduled, but they finished the job. Your task of rebuilding your life is quite similar and it would be advisable to take some encouragement from this illustration. This is no cheap pep talk, this is reality, this is practical, this is possible but you'll never find out unless you stick with the plan.

How do I know it's possible? I've been in situations where I felt weak and helpless, thinking it was the end of the world and that there was no hope. I woke up to the truth and acted on my desire for change. I experienced some of the worst times in my entire life during that period; I was plagued with extreme fear and anxiety, lost my self-confidence, my self-esteem. I lost cars and my home but I kept my head. I had to because there was a family to take care of and because I loved them I had to survive for them. My friend, I know what it's like to just be able to survive. It's almost like being barely alive. I was a broken man and yes at times I wanted to be buried in self-pity, walking around wearing paper smiles. I was too proud to let anyone see my sorrow and pain especially knowing how my life was before. Prior to my demise, I had a great job, a model family life, cars and a beautiful home. Yes I had the world on a string with the string wrapped tightly around my fingers, feeling really good about myself, and was well respected in and out of my circle. People looked up to me and that felt good. One of the things I enjoyed most was being able to help others; I trained people in life skills and self-esteem. Motivational speaking was one of the most rewarding things I did and enjoyed doing it often.

Daddy never told me.... No he never did because he wasn't around when I needed him and even if he was there doing Dad's stuff, it could not have prepared me for that experience. My point is, unless you are clairvoyant and can look into the future, nothing does quite a good enough job to prepare you for some of the unexpected things that can destroy your life. As badly as I felt at that time, I held myself together, for on top of the fears I was buried under, I was more afraid of totally losing my mind.

This is no pep talk. This is real, this is reality. There were many times that I wept bitterly, got angry at the world because the world was mean, unkind and grossly unfair. Oh yes, I was "fearfully mad at God." I tried all I thought I knew to rebound but I later realized that I didn't do it right. When one is in a desperate situation it is not unusual that you fumble and can make more mistakes. Then additional frustration sets in, creating a sense of defeat. It was like walking around in the dark. Hearing pep talk after pep talk made me feel better at times but much didn't change. It was like I was waiting for a miracle to happen, waiting for someone or something to come and deliver me from the mess.

At times we end up staying in a state of defeat for much longer than we should for different reasons. Mine lasted for over three years. One night it was like a light was turned on in my head and that was when I realized that I had to do something and do it urgently.

I:
Looked at my situation
Knew that I wanted change
Was willing to change
Wanted it badly
And was willing to seek help

During those three years of torture, my business was doing badly. The expenses were greater than the income and it was really rough. Interestingly enough while running the restaurant with very little coming in allowed me more time to spend with some of the few customers who came in from time to time. It would always be that the ones I was able to spend time with were always the ones dealing with issues. Surprisingly I found myself listening and encouraging these people. It was as if that was my mission. This went on throughout those very mean three years and for some reason I would walk away feeling a sense of fulfillment. More and more people came to the restaurant and like clockwork a familiar conversation would start and end the same way just like the others. To put the icing on the cake, quite a few of those persons I spoke with would return to tell me how encouraged they became because of our talks. Not only were they encouraged but also found solutions and were better off. I thought, wow, I sell Food for the Belly and Food for the Soul.

The morning of my awakening, I picked up the phone and called the CFO of the company I had most recently consulted for and without even knowing what I was going to say, the words just came out, "hey....How are you doing? Do you have a spot for a good man?" Without hesitation, he said, "for a good man, yes, when can you come down so we can talk?" That was my move and within three days I was back in my former position with a new and much better contract than before. I was back to being me, trampled on my fears, regained my self-confidence and Rebounded. Allow me to emphasize this. It wasn't all smooth sailing. It took effort and determination, self-encouragement and maintaining a Positive Mental Attitude, yes PMA. This is how I live my life today simply because I learned to change my mind set. Remember my friends, if it doesn't come in the time you expect or hope, keep at it, stay the course and stick with the plan.

Personal Notes:

Personal Notes:

Chapter 4

A New Way of Thinking

Making It Happen

My wish is not to make this a religious book or to give the impression that I'm preaching at you but we need to have a belief system and I would encourage you to believe in something that is good. Good has far reaching tentacles; I have heard many definitions of this fine virtue. Being honest about what I've discovered about us humans is that the greater percentage of us wants to be good. We want to do good. Ask anyone you know and even those who you don't know, "Are you a good person or do you believe that you're a good person?" And they will tell you "yes...at least I think so or I'd like to think so." But, what is good, and what does it mean to be good? What does good look like?

The story of David and the "Bad" Giant is remarkably interesting and can be looked at from several different angles or viewpoints. Hopefully, we will be able to look into this story and see what we find that will be helpful to us in our new way of thinking. For the most part, I hardly think that anyone actually enjoys seeing another person being oppressed and especially a nation or ethnic group. It becomes harder to handle if you are a part of such a group or have close ties with that group or nation. Those of us who are aware of current worldwide events are quite familiar with this kind of oppression and I'm sure will be able to understand this story more easily.

We Can Accomplish Much Through Determination

An average looking young man grew up in a remote area of his small country as a shepherd, tending flocks his family owned. While appearing to be of average demeanor, what sets him apart from the others (his older brothers) was his character and mindset. He was of a determined mind and would stop at nothing to protect the sheep in his care. On one occasion, he wrestled a lion to death to save his family's livelihood. Talk about bravery, a show of inner strength and self-confidence. He most likely didn't consider the danger in taking on the King of the Jungle; this might have been a stupid idea, obviously a risky one for sure.

What is the lion in your life today? How do you see this lion? There are several ways in which David could have responded, the most obvious would have been to run away to save his life. He could have hidden and yelled for help. Based on his size, he was not well-built as the others, or like Samson who also killed a lion (as is recorded). He was a small man with a Big Heart. Were his actions impulsive or was this really his nature to preserve life and integrity? How will you respond to the lion that's approaching or is standing staring you in the eyes and saying, "I'm bigger, stronger, and more powerful than you"? It doesn't seem like there was much of a fight but the result is that the lion was dead and the sheep were saved. It is said that he who fights and runs away, lives to fight another day...there is some truth to that, I agree, but David's actions in my opinion were a more direct approach. Running away would have resulted in a loss of what he was primarily intent on protecting. You may or may not have a family to protect, it might be your business, job or your self-esteem. Your primary responsibility is to protect you because if there's no you, there's no one to protect the rest. Remember that you are the most important part of this equation.

David's action proved the kind of person he was and showed what can be accomplished through determination when you're purposeful in your life's ambition. Throughout David's life, he lived with the knowledge of how his nation had been oppressed, the many attacks on his homeland, and the slaughtering of his fellow citizens. This deeply bothered him, and he couldn't wait for a chance to do something about it. The record showed that no one was prepared or willing to address the issue out of fear. Earlier, we talked about the effects of fear and the cost of fear, how destructive and defeating it is. The leadership of his nation had no idea what to do or how to handle the problem. Regardless of who you are, what you possess, where you've been in life, and your many achievements, it doesn't exclude you from life's challenges.

David finally got a chance to speak up about the oppression and what should be done but was dismissed and reprimanded because he was uneducated and inexperienced in such matters. However, he was determined to not just sit around and do nothing. Every time he tried to be heard, he was turned away and reminded of his position as just a keeper of sheep, which was among the most demeaning of occupations. In this case, he was being prevented from taking out the lion that oppressed his nation.

Finding Your Inner Strengths and Using Them

What is inside you can be more powerful than you can imagine. The day came when someone decided to listen to David, but with much reservation because they did not think that this young man could make any positive contribution to the worsening conditions. After much consideration and debate, he was given the go ahead to confront his second lion that came in the form of a nine foot giant who had a reputation of crushing anything in his path. The sight of him alone was enough to scare off an entire army (the record repeatedly showed this).

He was cautioned and warned of the threat to his own life but most importantly, the greater threat to the entire nation if his plan failed. Does this sound like something you've heard before? These negativities are designed to prevent progress and success; they will keep you from finding out what you're made of and what you can do. Don't let anyone tell you that you can't do what burns inside you, that ambition you've had for a while, that thing that consumes your passion. Follow that yearning and don't let fear throw you off track or discourage you.

So many have ended up with gross disappointments, and many have been driven to depression as a result of broken dreams and unattained goals. Explore all your potentials go after what's in your heart. Better to try and find out, rather than to never have tried at all. Being driven by his passion, David went out and defeated his giant; he permanently put an end to what would have turned out to be a total annihilation of his nation, family, and culture. Finding your strengths and using them for good will propel you to heights beyond your wildest imagination. You can rise from the lowest point in your life and be lifted to heights you never would have imagined. With such a show of confidence and bravery, the shepherd became king.

The contrast between good and bad is that good seeks out opportunities to preserve and protect what is meaningful and valuable. Bad, however, seeks to do the direct opposite of preserving and protecting life and values, the very elements that make life sacred and worth living. What is life worth without values and sacredness. No wonder some have resorted to a life of crime and cruelty. Our society is overrun with lewd and unprincipled behavior, and this is especially disappointing when it comes from the top. Just as an individual needs to revisit or find value in his life so does our society, which will in turn positively affect the world, making it a more pleasant place to live for our children and us. From the beginning of time there has been this battle between the forces of good and bad. It does appear at times like bad will prevail but not a chance of that happening. Love is and will always be stronger than hate. In the end, good will conquer evil and those of us who are on the side of good will rejoice and celebrate the win.

Spot Check (How are you doing?)

My hope is that at this moment, you're already encouraged and motivated, and that you have come to the realization that you are a winner. Have you told yourself that? Do you believe it? How will you know this? Think about it carefully. Get up and do something bold, that thing you're so disappointed about, give it another go. That thing you failed at doing; get up, make another go of it. This might be the time you will succeed, this time around could be your season, your time to flourish.

Maybe you didn't really fail at the things you attempted; maybe you just gave up too early for whatever reason. Now, it's time to reexamine the aim, goal, and regain the passion, and recall the enthusiasm you once had. Was it a career goal? Hey, it's never too late, you can always get requalified, go back to school, and take some classes. Was it a business ambition? Give some more thought to it or choose another idea that is more marketable. Did you become depressed because of a broken relationship? You might have been cheated on and your pride is hurt, your ego got crushed. Have you ever thought that the person who hurt you may not have been the right one for you? Believe me; it is totally possible to restart your engine. Believe in you; be encouraged, you're not dead yet. If you're young, there is a lot of living left to do; time is on your side. If you're older, pledge to live your best life to the end. Realize that a renewed you is a renewed life. Several studies have shown that improving your mental health can significantly add years to any life.

Personal Notes:

Personal Notes:

Chapter 5
The Way Forward
Moving Towards Success and Achieving It

Have you ever had your vehicle break down on your way to somewhere important? Does this sound familiar? I'm sure it does. It may not have been a break down. Maybe you were stuck in traffic for extremely long periods of time. Now, that's an ordeal that even the most patient person can never be comfortable with.

What a relief when traffic starts moving again. Now you're on your way to that important appointment and the anger you felt is gone. You're calmer, things are moving quietly, but then you remember, the appointment is at 11:30 am; it's now 11:00 am. You only have a half an hour to get there...you are 45 miles away. You start to panic, you start to tremble, and your right foot is shivering on the gas pedal. Then you start drowning in nervousness; you're sweating, hands are shaking. That clean shirt that you put on is now soaked; you loosen your tie and try to breathe, but you end up gasping for air......"what is going on....why is this happening?" "I can't believe this", you say. As a matter of fact, you yell it out loud and although the windows are up, you catch yourself and feel kind of weird because you wonder if the old lady in the lane on your left heard you. You notice a bunch of kids on the school bus in front of you, gathered at the rear window of the bus making faces, pointing and laughing... Oh boy....its 11:15, you're off the highway now but every traffic light turns red as you approach, 11:20 am and you try to pull yourself together. Just two more blocks to go,....I can make it you tell yourself, 11:26 am, now you're in the parking lot, out of the car you jump, half way to the door of the building, and then you realize that you left your portfolio in the car. "oh my God, what is going on?", you shout as you race back to the car. For a moment you fumble with the key fob, finally with portfolio in hand, you run to the reception desk and breathlessly announce yourself to the lady sitting there taking a message on the phone. She looks up at you as if to say "Have you no manners?" "Can't you see I'm on the phone." After what seemed like an eternity, she puts the phone down and ever so kindly said, "Sir, may I help you?" Are you in some kind of trouble?" Ashamed as you are you respond, "I'm Brian Trotter and I'm here to see Mr. Daniel Dayton." Oh...Mr. Trotter, you're somewhat late, have a seat while I see if Mr. Dayton is available. You might as well go to the men's room to freshen up.

Feeling like a real fool, you hurry to the restroom, staring in the mirror at yourself, "what a mess" you say and then wonder, is it worth going through with this? All the preparation, all the planning, the time and effort it took just to get this appointment and I'm late, I'm nervous, I'm a mess. As I walk out of the restroom not feeling all that great, Jen the receptionist, calls out, oh Mr. Trotter... you walk over to the desk trying hard to look composed and business like. She smiles and says "I just heard from Mr. Dayton. He sends his apology and asked if you would be willing to reschedule or wait approximately an hour. He got held up at another meeting." OMG... This is unbelievable, this is amazing, I thought, seriously... I still have a chance? So I pretend to be in control and find enough courage to answer "Well I...I do you have another presentation to do (which was an all-out lie) how about an hour and a half? Does that work? She said, "Yes", I say "that works." "Ok I'll arrange it, see you at 12:50." Ok, I'll see you then. At that moment if I wasn't in the lobby, I would be doing cartwheels, and jumping with excitement. All is not lost after all.

Staying positive is extremely hard to do at times. I know that for a fact, but on this journey it is a must. It's the only way to achieve the success you are going after; preparation is also very important. Always plan ahead giving yourself more than enough time to get to where you need to go. This will compensate for incidents such as what happened in Brian's case. Imagine if Mr. Dayton was waiting and Brian was late. Things could have gone the other way. No one likes to be kept waiting, and especially in situations such as this where competition is strong. So many people are after the same position or the same contract.

Most likely Brian would not be accommodated. Showing up late for this meeting is not acceptable.

Brian went to a cozy little cafe a block away, ordered a coffee and danish and took advantage of the time to regroup and put his thoughts in perspective. He went over his presentation in accurate detail several times before heading back to Daytona Enterprises. He was now more relaxed and felt quite ready. After meeting Mr. Dayton and giving what he thought was a good presentation, he left feeling as if he'd accomplished the task of the day, a very important one in his opinion. A few days later, the call came from Dayton Enterprises. Brian was invited to do a second presentation, this time with the board members present. It turned out to be the best day of his life. He was offered quite a lucrative contract.

The path to success will not be without upsets and setbacks. There will be hurdles and challenges to overcome. At times you'll get so close to your goal and something unexpected happens. Don't be thrown off track, don't start second guessing yourself, stay focused and keep moving forward. Just as Brian's determination kept him focused on winning that contract although there were setbacks and challenges, in the same manner keep going regardless of what is in your way.

It is vitally important to maintain constant focus on your ambitions to safeguard against distractions and discouragement. These will be sure to come about from time to time. Do sufficient research and plan your strategy. Be open to criticism and seek good advice especially from persons who are knowledgeable. This will give valuable information to help you in your planning.

Plan Ahead...Be Willing to Learn

Michael wanted to be an entertainer. He took acting, dancing, and singing lessons. He went as far as changing his facial appearance through plastic surgery and sculpted his body by going to the gym and having a personal trainer. He looked amazing. He was fortunate to land a few brief minor roles which were encouraging and of course made him feel like things were off to a good start. Obviously, "show biz" is a pretty uncertain and not so easy business and not everyone has the mental and emotional fortitude it requires to stick with it to achieve some measure of success or to excel.

While his dreams of being in the spotlight were at the forefront of his mind, he had a habit of being inconsistent and that plagued him. He looked the part but had great difficulty landing significant roles, and every time he did not get chosen, he would become discouraged and angry. The feeling of failure plagued him, but he kept going, which was good. The problem, however, was that he didn't handle criticism well and was not prepared to accept sound advice because he felt he was good enough or at times even better than others. I encourage you to take note that if the game isn't working for you, change the way you play the game. Everything is about attitude. It is dangerous not to have the right attitude concerning whatever you're doing. In many cases you may have to take baby steps. It may take longer than you hope or imagine. As I said earlier, the world of entertainment is tough and making advancements doesn't come about the same way for everyone.

There was a lot of money invested in this undertaking, a lot of time and quite a lot of yearning. Not seeing many possibilities here in America, like many aspiring entertainers, Michael decided to go to Europe in hopes of finding better opportunities. It was as if nothing changed, He hung out with the wrong crowd, those who took disadvantage of his lack of knowledge, and they made empty promises. He listened to what sounded good but lacked substance. In the interim more and more money was wasted but he never wanted to give up the dream he had, and that is commendable. The problem was that he didn't change the way he played the game.

Under such conditions, one needs to do some self-evaluation. If you want change, you have to be willing to change. You must decide how badly you want that change. Seek help if you can't figure things out on your own. Change your mindset or maybe try something new. There is nothing wrong with having more than just one goal in mind. You may sometimes need to switch your focus to something else. It is possible that you might do better at something else within the same field or in a different field. Keep in mind the principles of going after your passion, challenge yourself.

Sadly, for Michael, he eventually gave up on his pursuits, ending up a broken, depressed, angry man and developed several serious medical conditions. Life teaches us lessons every day and it is up us to recognize these lessons. It is up to us to be open-minded and learn. There is always the opportunity for second, third and even forth chances. The idea is to keep on trying until you get it right. Don't give up on your passion. You possess what it takes to accomplish the task ahead.

I find it so fascinating seeing elderly people, especially retirees who didn't finish high school or college, receiving their high school diploma or college degree very late in life. It makes me wonder why, why at this late stage of life? The reason in most cases is that it was a goal, a must have, it gave a sense of completion, a feeling of accomplishment. It was a passion, a life's goal. These folks were determined not to die without reaching this important milestone. They lived into their seventies, eighties and beyond having had a good life but didn't give up on finally achieving the goal they've had all those years. Consider your current situation. It may be much more crucial than those; the level of urgency may be greater. It might be the reason you're so unhappy, frustrated, depressed or unfulfilled. Think about it. Don't continue to let obstacles keep you from a fulfilled life. Change the game or the way you play the game. The time to take control is now, not tomorrow. The time to move ahead is right now; there's no time to waste, get on the train, it's pulling out, say bye bye to failure.

I had a conversation with a lady from Eastern Europe. I met her some years ago while on a job consultation. We have since become fairly good friends. I love spending time with her, especially listening to her collection of fascinating stories. One story in particular, stood out because it fits in quite well with the main focus of this book. Let me say, that I have no way of verifying the facts of this very touching story, however, I'd like to share it with you. The story is about a young girl, who, in her early years was training to be a gymnast and a ballerina. We know that is a common pastime and a passion on that side of the world. Her family wasn't quite able to financially support the costly lessons, but she worked hard at her routines both as a budding gymnast and an aspiring ballerina. This paid off in the way of her winning several competitions and won her scholarships to some of the most prestigious academies. Irina was on her way and of course was doing exceptionally well. She was only just so close to her goal of becoming an acclaimed professional and then tragedy hit. Her accident was not life threatening, there was hope for her recovery, but then came severe political unrest in her country which resulted in an "attempted over throw" of the government. This unfortunate event interrupted her recovery and therapy due to the ongoing desperate state of affairs in the country.

Eventually it turned out that after several years the opportunities to continue her participation in Sports and Dance had passed. This was devastating and quite a blow to her dreams. She went through a very rough time and depression set in. For a number of years she was subdued and felt helpless and somewhat hopeless. Then one night while lying in bed wondering what to do, and how to fight her way out of depression and hopelessness, it was as if someone flipped a switch and the light came on. That's when she knew all was not lost. After all those years of nothingness and emptiness, feeling hopeless and robbed by life's circumstances, thinking of the greed, envy and the selfishness of one group wanting power and control, the number of and senseless loss of life and structural destruction to what was once a peaceful county, it happened for her, "yes", she said out loud..."Yes, that's what I'll do, I will teach young girls how to dance and be gymnasts."

She could not wait for the morning, for the sun to rise. For the next several hours she thought, and ideas just kept coming to her in terms of how to go about launching this new and exciting adventure. She grabbed a notepad that sat on the circular metal nightstand by her wood framed full size bed which she shared with her younger sister. Irina wrote and wrote, and everything that came to her mind during those hours was written down. With very little money in her purse she headed to town, to the corner store where there was a copy machine. You see, she had written a hand-made flyer and attached an old photo that was taken at one of her award winning performances. As she entered the store, her hands were literally frozen from the cold of that brutal winter. She heard someone shout "It's Irina Slevoski." Suddenly she was surrounded by the few patrons in the store. Everyone was so happy to see her. They expressed grief at her loss, compliments at her achievements and joy at seeing her again.

The middle aged man who shouted out her name, asked "What is that in your, hand, may I see?" After reading it aloud and the cheering and applause had finally died down, he asked her, "Do you have a place to open your school? When will you start? Can I help you advertise?" He led her to his small office in the back of the store where they talked for quite a long time. Not to bore you with all the details, but things worked out in such a miraculous way. Her school was opened in that very building and was successful. She and the owner were married a few years later. Her beloved husband died fifteen years after their marriage and that was when she migrated to America. Today Irina is as happy as anyone could be, always smiling and beaming with joy. It is always a pleasure to spend time with my friend, listening to many other stories. She usually has a story to share.

Quite a moving story, wouldn't you say? This young woman rebounded to a life of contentment, even though her original ambitions were prevented due reasons beyond her control. She forged ahead and achieved her goal. I believe it is worth mentioning that there is something to be gained from inspiring stories, whether fact or fiction. Many of us will agree that in addition to the reading pleasure these types of stories provide, there's also valuable takeaways and lessons to be learned.

Please, would you stop just for a moment and let this sink in. There is always a way out of any demise. Yes you can make that change, yes you can rebound. It is never too late. Start hoping again; maintain hope, and hold on. It may be a rough ride when starting out, but hold on to hope and with determination.... Move ahead.

Develop a Belief System
Believe in something bigger than yourself

So you may say, "I don't believe in anything or anyone but myself." Well my friend, let's face it....if that were the truth, then you wouldn't be where you are now. You would have had things under control. One is only entitled to say that when one has developed positive control over one's personal life. Still that's not a bad way to feel or think, but be sure you're fully equipped to go it alone. No matter how capable and in control we think we are, there's something or someone bigger and better than we are. Do the research. There are many Entrepreneurs and Professionals who are strong believers in certain life principles which enabled them to succeed. You won't hear me telling you or making suggestions as to what you should choose to believe in but I will suggest that whatever you choose it should be something greater than anything you've ever believed in. Make it something bigger, stronger, more disciplined, something you can be guided by. Believe in something that will bring about change and make you a better person.

Religion, in my opinion, is the most sought after and subscribed to belief system in the world. I find it most interesting that New Age and Eastern Religions including Mysticism are extremely popular among westerners. Many famous and well accomplished people are deeply dedicated to such beliefs. Millions are seeking desperately for something to hold on to and something to hold on to them. For those of us who are not rich and famous, it's hard to understand why the accumulated wealth of the aforementioned is not and never seem to be enough to bring contentment.

I think of how traditional western religions seem to be going out of style or existence, I've noticed how these people who have transitioned to eastern belief systems have developed a dedicated sense of discipline toward life, work, family, community etc. Change is good. Note that when I refer to change, it will always be change for the good and better. Hopefully, you are not thinking that I'm advocating for any religion. It's just that this is very noticeable to me, and I find it extremely remarkable and worthy of mentioning. Our traditional western religions are also worthwhile mentioning. I see dedication and commitment from people of this persuasion, going to church, attending mass, bible studies etc. The evidence is also in their life style. Many are and will forever be faithful to their beliefs and that is admirable, I will say...if it makes you a better person, by all means hold on to it. There's good in most things. We just have to find the good that lies there. Interestingly though, not many people are aware of the fact that sometimes we need to go beyond the surface and dig deep to find the valuable essence of fulfillments.

There are those who have a scientific belief system and that's ok. Good also exists in this infinite way of thinking and the results are astounding. Our technological believers are to be commended for the many technological advancements. We all have benefited from modern technology and will continue to do so. Sometimes it's frightening to think of what is to be unveiled next. We have learned so much about space, the planets, new galaxies are being discovered. We now know more about life and our very existence. Scientific believers think in terms of probability, positivity and relativity. These are strong and important building blocks for the foundation of a good life. As I have said and will keep saying, it all happens in the mind. It was the way of thinking that had you in bondage for years. Now it's time to use your mind to free yourself and maintain that freedom.

Whether you were born whole, with all your faculties fully functional or born with physical deficiencies, this does not include serious mental health issues, we all have a natural instinct to survive. How we follow that instinct is entirely up to us and we can all realize our ambitions and move ahead to a place of contentment and satisfaction. The way forward is now in front of you. Now you decide how you will proceed. Again I emphasize, believe in something bigger and better than yourself. Be bold, be brave, and be willing to take chances. Set your goals, go after them with everything you got, seek help, be open to new ideas, seek good advice, and for sure you'll get there. Don't be discouraged. Be patient but approach it with a sense of urgency.

Procrastination is not wise. "Don't put off for tomorrow, what you can do today." I found this to be a very true statement. It is somewhat a part of our nature and believe me, I know how it goes. But make no mistake that this bad habit can take a strong hold in your life. Many projects have been left undone, not started, many tasks have gone past due and many goals not realized simply because of procrastination. According to Psychology Today, procrastination is evaluated in this way... "Everyone puts things off sometimes, but procrastinators chronically avoid difficult tasks and may deliberately look for distractions. Procrastination tends to reflect a person's struggle with self-control. For habitual procrastinators, who represent nearly 20 percent of the population....'I don't feel like it' come to take precedence over their goals or responsibilities and can set them on a downward spiral of negative emotions that further deter future efforts." "Procrastination also involves a degree of self-deception. At some level, Procrastinators are aware of their actions and the consequences, but changing their habits requires even more effort than completing the task in front of them" (Psychologytoday.com, 2022). It's dangerous to sit where you have been sitting throughout your struggle for change and not do something proactively and with a sense of urgency. Let's change the narrative, transform the perception, and prevent the consequences. The habit of procrastination can be quite costly. I'm sure you know that, I know that, I had to learn that, and I learned it the hard way. Make the decision to step forward, step out and start the change.

Remember my friends, you have pulled yourself out of the "no can do" way of thinking. You've made the decision to move ahead, you want change and you're on your way. Do not get side tracked by surrendering to the temptation to procrastinate. For too long you were lying dormant in fear and lack of self-confidence. You have come too far to stop or regress. Your life is about to take off. Ambitions, dreams, goals and renewals are right there within reach. Go ahead, reach out and grab hold of it. This is your big moment, your moment to grow, to blossom, to win.

Adopt a Mentor Strategy
Someone or Something to Look up to
(See strategies on pages 194-196)

According to research, 84% of Fortune 500 hundred companies have mentoring programs (mentorloop.com, 2024). When looking for success, mentoring programs now hold a permanent fixture in today's workforce. How fascinating and eye opening is this information! I found that most extremely successful people adopted a mentoring program. Whether it was an actual organized program in which they were actively involved, a particular individual with whom they connected or maybe they just observed someone from the sidelines. Some people get their motivation from following certain individuals on social media. Undeniably, this strategy is of great value and is bound to produce rewarding results if adhered to, and if the individuals are chosen wisely.

I listen to many people who talk about sports all the time and I have always admired the commitment and dedication they have to their favorite team or their sports hero. Funny enough I've heard and seen these interactions become quite heated to the point where they almost got physical. Some have resulted in real fist fights. Absolutely nothing is wrong with all that dedication and enthusiasm. I think, however, that it should be done in the spirit of good, respectful, sportsmanship. The problem with such attitudes from those who end up in an unpleasant argument, is that a lot of the individuals don't have their lives under control yet they expend all that effort into defending their favorite player or beating up on those they don't like. I ask myself, to what benefit? We can almost safely say that the majority of professional sports players have made remarkable strides in their live and their career. They achieved their goals; now it's your turn to achieve yours.

My advice to everyone reading this book, is to harness all that energy, enthusiasm, and dedication, and channel them towards your recovery process. Do not waste precious time on things and involvement that are of no benefit to improving your life and movement towards your goals.

Just as it is important to believe in something or someone bigger and better than yourself, it is equally important to have something or someone to be mentored by, to pattern, to look up to. As studies have shown, an overwhelming number of persons who are already doing quite well have recognized the need to become more accomplished. They see the sky as the limit. They are aware of the endless possibilities, and are doing something about it. They sought to be mentored. We're all aware of what it takes to be a part of such a prestigious group, Fortune 500...we can refer to these companies as overachievers, and that's exactly what they are. The difference however is that they want change, and are willing to change, and ultimately they sought help, adopting a mentoring program.

Now let's talk about you. You're down and depressed, fearful, lacking self-confidence, no drive, and life is miserable. You feel like there's no point in trying. You may even feel like trying won't help. Here are some valuable tips to get you going. Remember, it starts with that first step, maybe baby steps. Find someone or something to be mentored by, someone to emulate, someone to help and encourage you, and most of all take the advice and run with it. Learn the lessons. These valuable tips were mentioned earlier. It's about repetition, and practice, doing it over and over until you get it right like learning to drive requires repeating the process until it becomes effortless. Not many people become discouraged to the point where they totally give up on perfecting the skill of driving. While becoming a proficient driver is very important, and extremely beneficial, this skill does not make you a better person. It puts you in control of the automobile but not in control of your emotions or your life for that matter.

If you can make all that effort towards becoming a qualified driver, why not do the same for the things you want to change in your life. Identify those deep issues that have set you back and have you bound and restricted. Use the same principles of determination and dedication to regaining control of your life. Again, I'll emphasize, "It doesn't matter how much you want change." If that first step is not made you will never move from where you are. It's like having the tools to complete an essential task and not using them the way they should be used to get the desired results.

My friends, I will continue to encourage you to take a positive stand against whatever is robbing you of the life you want to live and enjoy. Don't let these negative thoughts and feelings destroy you and steal your chances of realizing your full potential. Step up and step out of the defeated, the destitute life you have been enduring for so long. Always keep in your mind that change is possible and it will come about with determination, dedication, and perseverance.

A FEW INTERESTING QUOTES

A little progress each day adds up to big results

Failure is a part of life, if you don't fail, you don't learn if you don't learn, you'll never experience change

Don't panic and work yourself in a frenzy, when you relax, your brain works best

The key to your happiness is within you

A bad attitude is like a flat tire, you cannot go anywhere until you change it

Don't lose hope; you might be closer to your breakthrough than you think

Change your Social environment, Change your Life

Be happy not because everything is good, see good in everything

Don't be afraid to take risks, if you win you'll be happy

If you lose, you'll be wise

Personal Notes:

Personal Notes:

Personal Notes:

Chapter 6
Are We There Yet?
Depending on where you want to go...

When setting goals, you should keep in mind that these goals or goal must be realistic and achievable. Be sure not to confuse pursuing your full potential and exceeding your own expectations, with setting achievable goals. Why did I say that, you ask? The expectation is that after reading and applying the simple practices (presented in this book) you will have learned that anything is possible if you put your mind to it. That's if you are determined and are prepared to do what is necessary. "Then the sky is the limit." Still, there is nothing wrong with starting with something reasonable and building on it as you go along. Depending on where you want to go and what you want to achieve, or prove to yourself and others, I still maintain that all things are possible with the right attitude.

At this point, I believe that many of you are ready and highly motivated, buzzing, and quite ready to go. I sincerely commend you and am extremely proud of you. Whatever your goal is, get a move on; there's no time like the present. As the saying goes, "strike while the iron is hot." Your readiness is an indicator that the journey has begun; the new you is here. So how does it feel my friends, after years of wanting a new life?

You may have suffered from one of the following:

Agoraphobia - Fear of being out in public or place and situations that may cause panic etc.

Monophonic - Fear of being alone

Anxiety - Fear about everyday situations

Lack of self-confidence – Fear of failure

Being an underachiever – Fear of pursuit of life goals

Being overweight – Fear of getting fat

Broken relationship – Fear of getting hurt

Depression – Fear of mental breakdown

These are just a few of the many issues that people face that have kept them in a miserable, hopeless existence. Far too many have experienced the negative, far reaching effects of these life challenges.

How does it really feel to know that you have found a way out? Do you feel free? Are you feeling like a load has been lifted from your shoulders? Stand up, straighten those shoulders, come into the sunshine, wake up and say "Hello World, it is I and I'm back." Embrace the new you. Remember those who told you that you couldn't recover, that you wouldn't recover. Some have said you're lazy, and no good, they said you'd never get better. This is a new day. I said new because for too long you have been thinking and saying "some old, same old, stuff." Now your eyes are opened and you are enlightened. Now you see things differently; you have a new perspective. Don't look back. Isn't it amazing how changing your mindset changes everything? And did you also know that if you do something continuously for eighteen days it becomes a habit? That is a good way to start creating good habits that will assist you in being consistent with your new way of thinking. Keep on reaffirming good thoughts about yourself, what you are doing and what you want to do.

I have also learned the importance of constantly working on myself, working on my weaknesses and maximizing the areas where I'm strong. We are not always strong in every area of our lives. That is why it is so important to be able to identify and know our strengths and weaknesses. While encouraging you to be proactive in identifying these abilities, you must seek to bring about a balance to become more well-rounded. Having balance will minimize the chance that your weaknesses will cause you to doubt your potential. Anyone can analyze their overall abilities, but if you're not sure what those are or may be, it is advisable to ask someone trustworthy and truthful, someone who will be honest with you and give positive feedback. You will find that among the most successful people are those who are willing to seek advice and listen to feedback.

Have you considered where you want to go and exactly what you want to achieve? What habits you want to change and what habits you need to adopt? Exactly what do you want to change about you that you're not happy with? You must be specific about this, otherwise you might be all dressed up with nowhere to go, or just spinning your wheels. Having a desire or desires without having a destination is pointless and will produce nothing. Your mission at this point is not to be searching in the dark. It should be having a clear vision of the path to bringing change and breaking free from whatever had you trapped. Remember, the "same old same old" is now a thing of the past. This is a new day with possibilities and opportunities you have longed for and wanted so badly. Step into the newness of the day and grab hold of what you were afraid to touch. Embrace it, take advantage of it, get your slice of the pie or go get the whole pie if that's what you want. Maximize the motivation you now have, do it without fear. If you make mistakes don't feel bad. Everyone makes mistakes. Go back and correct them and keep moving ahead. Be prepared to fight discouragement and don't be stopped by hurdles. Be proud of you every time you overcome discouragement and pat yourself on the back when you clear a hurdle. Celebrate every accomplishment however small. That's the fuel to your fire. It serves only to energize the efforts you've made and boost your drive towards taking down the next duck in the row.

This is not rocket science. These are simple practical exercises that will take you to heights beyond your imagination. It is in you, and was always there. You probably didn't believe it was or didn't know you had it in you. Realize that you are worthwhile, that you are capable, that you can and will accomplish what you set out to do.

I can see you now, just look at you...Amazing, Awesome. You have come a long way from where you were for as long as you were there. Now there should be nothing stopping you from moving forward. Regardless of what you may encounter, do not get distracted. Keep those goals in the forefront of your mind; you are on the most important mission of your life.

When I was a teenager, I read a book about thinking positively. Having read that made an enormous difference in my life. Yes, I was energized. I was feeling good about myself; I had hope and high expectations. I saw everything in a different light. It is not unusual for this to happen to people whether it's a book, a seminar, or a motivational speaker. Many people become temporarily motivated and excited. They get on a high which is short lived. This happens quite frequently and in the end, they feel let down and fall back into the stagnation of a negative mind set making it so much harder to navigate their way out. My mistake, however, was that every time I hit a snag in my plans, I got thrown off track and eventually stopped trying. Looking back at that experience many years later, I realized what went wrong in the process and took responsibility for my failures. It was like offering food to a hungry man but he does not eat because he didn't like what he was given. During those years I wanted change but was not willing to go as far as I needed to go or do what was necessary to effect change. Let's just say that I was half way there. After being energized and motivated, after taking that first step, I ignored the fact that there would be hurdles and discouragement along the way. My expectation was that things should go smoothly on my way to reaching my goals, but I did not take the simple practical steps I'm now sharing with you.

So are we there yet? Only you will know the answer to that question. You are the only one who really knows the truth about who you are. Regardless of having a coach or a trainer, it is totally up to you to measure the degree of your progress and success. Only you know exactly how you feel about yourself at this point in your quest for change compared to where you were before you started. Now that you've become more open minded and have prepared yourself for what's ahead, challenge yourself every day to accomplish something productive. Do not procrastinate; prove to yourself that you will be better off by doing the thing you don't feel like doing at the time it should be done. I guarantee you that you will indeed feel better when it is done as opposed to not having done it and having to worry about doing it some other time.

Try not to take on too much too early or at one time. Give yourself space and sufficient time to properly complete each task. Doing so will eliminate complications and simplify the process. Be especially purposeful regarding the expected results. This will help in maintaining your focus. I want to say just a bit more about maintaining your focus because I find that if this is not a constant, you will be left vulnerable to distractions and lose your momentum. So far we have repeatedly referred to the need for consistency by way of cultivating good habits and that everything comes at a cost. You will have to give up things in your life that have become routine, to make way for incorporating these best practices. Let's start with those things which lack importance and offer no value to your well-being. Consider those things which seem to happen by default. They are in most cases, thoughts, attitudes and, yes, habits. For instance, if your goal is to improve your social skills, a good place to start would be to work on your ability to communicate with people. Start where you feel comfortable.

Try getting to know what they like to talk about, what their interests are, the subjects and issues that are most important to them. People have varying interests. Some are things like their children. Ask about their age, school, things of that nature, and if you have children, share with them about yours also. You can do the same on the subject of sports. If their interests are things you don't know anything or not much about, ask relevant questions. Avoid debating at all cost and try to formulate your questions in a way that encourage good responses. Be complimentary and pleasant. This is a good opportunity to exercise the best practices you used to build your self-confidence.

Learn to make yourself look presentable. Your appearance does say a lot about you, I'm not referring to fashion even though it might be necessary in some cases to make some adjustments where that is concerned. After coming such a long way and having worked on your self-esteem and self-confidence, go out and be the best you can be. Conduct should be socially acceptable when trying to build friendships and connecting with new people. By now you should have migrated from, or suspended the former social environment you were in, the one that didn't do much or anything for that matter to contribute to you becoming a better you. Smiling is contagious, as the song says "when you're smiling, the whole world smiles with you." This is very true. Be yourself, but always be pleasant, "…put on a happy face." No one wants to be around sad and grumpy people. Be confident but not overbearing. You don't want people to be turned off by that. Again these are a few simple practical tips.

Surround yourself with everything that's relevant to your focus, people, literature, documentaries, whatever will make a valuable contribution to keeping you on track and keeping you motivated. Embrace it. These practices must become priority as opposed to everything else that offers no value and is of no benefit to you. Think, and if necessary meditate on your ambitions daily. Be consistent. Be reminded that there are no wrong answers. Your progress is very personal and you should pace yourself based on the severity of your situation. Not everyone is capable of mastering new habits at the same pace. We have varying capacities and competence.

The idea is, when rebuilding a broken life, it takes well invested time, sincere effort, determination, consistency and maintaining your focus. All these will require patience and tolerance. It will not happen overnight. You will have to give up somethings that may be hard to leave behind.

If your responses to the questions below are positive in contrast to the way you previously lived your life, then you have succeeded in your quest for change.

At this point, you might want to do a progress check:

Ask yourself these questions, and be sure to answer them with honesty

1. How differently do I feel about myself?

    Answer _____

2. What changes have I implemented in regards to my previous way of thinking?

   Answer _____

3. How will I measure my progress?

   Answer _____

4. Have I been using the suggested best practices consistently?

   Answer _____

5. The most valuable thing I've learned so far, is?

   Answer _____

6. Am I satisfied with my progress?

   Answer _____

7. Am I seeing my desired results?

   Answer _____

Personal Notes:

Personal Notes:

Chapter 7
Stop and Smell the Roses

Fascinating that even at my age, I find that I reflect on my childhood quite frequently remembering the days when I didn't have a care in the world. Everything was beautiful. It was almost continuous laughter and playfulness. That however was before I came to understand life as it really was. I realized that mom and dad had issues, I recognized the importance of sufficient parental attention and mad that money was of great importance to properly maintain a family, a large family. It was at a very young age, when most kids my age were still laughing and playing without a care in the world, when the reality of my family became apparent and it diminished the laughter and playfulness significantly.

William started his reflection of his childhood with the friends he went on a fishing trip with when they stopped at Sam's Bar and Grill which was on the other side of the road from a rest stop. There he saw several families pulled in to refresh themselves from a long drive. Some families obviously were on a traveling vacation, some just a weekend drive, there were U-Haul vans, trailers, RV's, mini vans and so on. They were sitting around one of the outdoor tables under a huge blue and white umbrella waiting for the waitress to bring out the large amount of food four strong men between the ages of 35 to 42 years of age would consume. They had spent hours on the lake fishing and although they brought the usual snacks, they were hungry.

Will, however seemed somewhat preoccupied and Rob, dubbed the therapist in this group of best buddies, asked, "Hey man. You had the biggest catch today. Why so glum?" It took Will quite a few seconds to respond. Hey, I just got carried away watching those families pulling in and out of the rest stop and especially seeing the kids playing without a care in the world. Fascinating, isn't it? Will is a strong, five feet eight inch guy of average built, clean shaven with a crew cut that he kept from being in the Marine Corp. He was an explosive specialist and mechanical engineer. Currently he is a private contractor, owning the company and working for the US Department of Defense. On that sunny summer Saturday waiting with his friends, he continued the story of growing up in a less than perfect home. He never actually told his friends about the issues he encountered and the hardship of growing up in dysfunctional family. He mostly talked about his late teen years just before joining the Marine Corp. Since leaving the Corp, he got married and is a proud father of eight year old twin boys, Charles and Cory, who he talks about often.

As I was saying before, half of my childhood was stolen from me in a manner I didn't understand. It forced me to become a man too early. I had to do things a more mature person should be doing. For instance, I didn't enjoy being in school most of the time. The fact that my parents had separated and my Mom was left with the responsibility of raising six children on her own made it unhappy for her, myself and my siblings. It was difficult, hard for her and hard for us. This meant there was less for everyone. Instead of being able to focus on my education, I was more concerned about working to support myself and help where I could and when I could. Then there was the lack of parental involvement in our lives. There was very little interaction because she worked most of the time. There was a lump in my throat and chest every time I would see families or visit with my friends who had both parents. That was a lot to deal with at that age. There was some good that came out of that experience though. I learned a lot about family life and responsibility. I learned about home making, going food shopping and most importantly, the will not only just to survive but also to be the best I could be.

With limited finances and less than perfect GPA, I had little chance and choices when it came to thinking about college, so I decided to join the army. That was my way out. I wasn't a tough guy, never even had a fight in my life. In the Marine Corps, he laughed out loud, I didn't even know I could shout. Guys, you know, it was a long, long, road, especially being on your own, but here I am today, married to a loving wife, two great kids and owning a great company. I made it. I'm happy, fulfilled and thankful, I'd be greedy if I wanted or asked for more than I have accomplished.

These days, I'm happy seeing families together, especially seeing children at play and hearing their laughter. I can relax and really enjoy my life. For all that I went through, which is a lot more than I've told you, it's great to be able to stop and smell the roses. Life is wonderful, a loving family, great company and the best friends any guy could ask for.

Where are we now? This is the question you need to answer for yourself, on your terms. Yes, you had it really hard. You fought with every ounce of strength you had. Things are different now and you can say you're a winner. It's time to enjoy the rest of your life. It is very true that there are many successful people in the world who are not quite happy. They are not enjoying their success and the life they worked so hard to build. That's not healthy at all.

It is time to celebrate your accomplishments. You need time for you. Be very thankful for where you now are and enjoy the results of your hard work. We've heard the term workaholics. They are those who bury themselves very deeply in their work. There are many reasons why some people are workaholics. For some it's a form of escape. The escape may be due to loneliness. They have no one to go home to and no other major responsibilities so in order to avoid being bored or otherwise unoccupied, they'll stay late on the job or take work home if they can. In this case I see nothing wrong with doing so. It's better to stay busy than to have too much time on your hands not knowing what to do with it. Others use this form of escape just as some use alcohol, to numb some sort of turmoil. For a number of people, it's hard to let go because they micromanage everything. They feel that sense of responsibility and think they are the only ones who can ensure that the job is done the way they think it should. I thoroughly believe in hard work and will in no way discount the efforts that are put into making sure the job is done properly. I commend all who have put extra effort into their pursuits.

What do I mean by stopping to smell the roses? Well my friends, I'm referring to reducing and preventing stress. For those who use work as an escape from loneliness, I would strongly recommend finding activities that will keep your mind active and stimulated, something that will bring you into contact with others who are very good company. It is not healthy for anyone to isolate themselves even if it seems like it is the appropriate thing to do. Being alone can be both physically and mentally unhealthy. I find that most people who have isolated themselves did it because of disappointment in friends, family or personal relationships.

I have seen it and I can tell you it is not a pleasant thing to see. I related the story of Michael who had his dreams of becoming an entertainer shattered. Although it was mostly his fault, the result is quite the same. After his downfall, he found it hard to go back to the community where he lived before his decision to try to find opportunities in Europe. The people he knew that were aware of his plan would be there to see him return empty handed. He also needed an income due to the huge financial loss he'd suffered. He had to find another job, which he did, but the shame and disappointment he felt, after having been literally robbed, caused him not trust anyone anymore. This of course was a tough place to be. Gradually, he gave up on people to the point where he had no friends or even social acquaintances. He distanced himself from even family members and blamed others for his loss. How very sad is that for anyone to resort to such a way of existing. "No man is an Island...No man stands alone."

His situation is not in the least unique. There is a large number of humans who are just existing. They are empty and lonely, sad and broken hearted with nothing to live for. So once again, I say to the lonely hearted, reach out and seek out good and caring people with whom you can associate and interact. It is healthy.

Here's a tip for those who feel that they can't let go so they spend more time doing more than they have to. I spent ten years in retail, from the sales floor to becoming a supervisor and then on to management. As a supervisor I learned that if my staff knew how to properly do their jobs, then my job became easier and it certainly did after I gave them sufficient training. Moving up management level, it wasn't rocket science to understand that if the supervisors knew how to do what I did, then not only did my job become easier but also those supervisors are now empowered. When you empower the people below you in rank, they feel valued and important. Morale grows, when morale is high, employees are happier and happy employees are more productive. A company or business will grow at an amazing pace when that company or business has happy and engaged employees.

I worked for one of America's largest leading electronics retailer and that was exactly how I was able to consistently reach and exceed my monthly goals. Through training and motivation that particular branch climbed to the top ten of over four hundred branches. I had much less stress, more respect and a very happy, motivated and engaged staff. I was able to stop and smell the roses. Let's learn to work smart. This is the only life you have. Don't you want to be around to enjoy it? You most certainly should. Life is too short to waste it with worry and unnecessary stress. It shouldn't be all work. Find time to relax and replenish yourself, body, soul and spirit. Let me say again, you deserve it, every bit of it.

We all won't become financially wealthy, but we can most definitely become wealthy in spirit, peace of mind, contentment, having a happy heart, a healthy body, and a wholesome life. Money is very important but it's not everything. There are millions of financially well off individuals who are extremely miserable and unhappy. They have everything money can buy but they are empty; something is missing. They don't have peace of mind. They're not experiencing contentment. Some are suffering from insomnia and other unpleasant issues like substance abuse. Dependence is a very common problem because there's a void they're trying to fill, the craving for the satisfaction which seems to constantly elude them.

Don't be caught in that trap. Choose to build your life on things that are more valuable, fulfilling and contribute to your spiritual, physical and mental well-being. Continue to maintain your self-respect and a sense of pride in whom you are and what you have accomplished. Do not let your success go to your head. Your past should only be a reminder of how far you've come and how much you have achieved. Your story can be of great motivation to others. Never look down on someone who's going through hardship.

At this point after coming such a long way and having accomplished so much as far as reaching or getting close to your main goals, your focus should be on you and maintaining the good habits and the best practices you have developed. Keep in mind that these behaviors are what brought you to where you currently are and that they will get you very far. In fact, they will get you to places beyond what you can imagine. Continue to work on your social, professional and personal skills. You can't afford to have come so far and then fall short, simply because you lose your momentum. Make time to relax and refresh yourself when feeling overwhelmed. Keep your mind and thought process healthy. Exercise as often as you can; as a matter of fact employ routine. If you like lifting weights, join a gym or if you prefer privacy and your own pace, buy your own equipment. Start walking running or swimming if you're not into intensive workouts. How about gardening, I find it to be extremely relaxing. Reading is a most powerful activity; it broadens the intellect and exercises the mind. Take up martial arts and meditation. They will keep you alert. You'll always be calm but in ready mode.

Try things (activities) that you have never done before. Dare to step out into the unknown.

All these will significantly contribute to lowering and controlling stress and keep you in a more relaxed and controlled state of being. Remember, you will accomplish a lot more and make better informed decisions when you're in a calm state of mind.

I honestly do congratulate you on all your achievements and developing the will to continue moving forward towards being the best you can be.

Personal Notes:

Personal Notes:

Personal Notes:

Chapter 8

Lend a Hand

Be Continuously Grateful

We all at some point in our lives have received help from someone and for this we all should be thankful. It is common courtesy to say "thank you" when someone offers help however small or simple. Have you ever just said 'thank you' but didn't really mean it? Have you really thought about the value of those two words? Thank you! That is common courtesy and should be extended to the person who out of the kindness of their heart offers help. It should be a part of everyone's make up to be grateful to the helper. Remember, they didn't have to do what they did for you.

Regardless of whether you believe in God or the Bible, regardless of whether you're religious or not, every religion teaches us to practice and live in a state of gratitude. Our parents taught us to be kind. We were taught that in school also. Then it shouldn't be a big deal, right? While you should be proud of your achievements through all the efforts and sacrifices you made in regards to rebuilding your life, be grateful for the fact that you are no longer where you were.

Kindness should be a new acquired habit of yours. It doesn't take anything away from you, and on the contrary, it adds to your life. During the worst year of my personal life when my restaurant was struggling, I was concerned about the people I saw who were in need of food. I came up with the idea of a soup kitchen. With the help of a few kind hearted, caring people, we started a soup kitchen once a week, every week. In addition, we collected clothing and gave to those who needed it. In addition to the soup kitchen and clothing, it was not unusual for me to give meals to some on a regular basis, not because I was able to afford to do so but out the kindness of my heart. The reward for me was that I was able to help someone who needed help and it didn't matter if they didn't show gratitude. It wasn't just a good feeling; there was a sense of fulfillment. Many days it felt better than when my daily income goals were met. I remember relating this to someone I knew and his response was "man ....you must be crazy."

The Good You Do Will Come Back to You

Do not show kindness to others for the sake of receiving kindness in return. Don't give with the hope of getting something back. The law of giving subsequently takes care of that. It is an indisputable fact. I have proven it time and time again. Try it and you'll see that it's true. You might not realize when it happens, but at some point in time, good just keeps coming your way in many forms. You may say "boy I'm lucky" not understanding the reality of what is happening. Doors are opening, you come in favor with people, the right people. Your whole life will change. Peace, contentment and happiness overwhelm your state of being. These are the rewards of kindness. It takes nothing away from an individual to be kind and show kindness to others. In fact, it adds to your life. Since kindness is not about looking for anything in return, just be kind, Period.

We talked about inspiring stories earlier, and again not to talk religion, but one of the most empowering stories I've read is actually from the Bible, the same writings most other civil laws are modeled after. This is about kindness without discrimination.

A man was traveling a long way on business. He noticed someone very badly hurt in a ditch on the side of the road. He stopped to have a look. He saw that the man was very badly beaten. Not only was he badly beaten but also he was robbed of his valuables. Immediately, without fear or questioning, the business man attended to the injured man's wounds. More likely than not, the business man had a first aid kit from which he was able to provide some medication and bandages. He realized how serious the injuries were and decided that this wounded man should not be left alone. He picked up the man and put him on his horse, carried him to a place where he could be cared for. Remarkably he didn't just leave the wounded man there. He gave money to the owner for the care of the patient. He also promised to stop by on his return to check on the wounded man and would be willing to pay any extra cost that was incurred for additional care. Honestly, is that more than remarkable? This was literally unheard of in those days but would be greatly applauded in today's society. There is however another side and other factors that make this more interesting and outstanding. Let's look at these factors in more detail.

In those days, there were many strict laws and ordinances concerning the mixing of races. Even within races there existed several different sects and classes in terms of hierarchy and so on. The wounded man was from one of the most despised groups in that particular society. There was not supposed to be interaction of any kind with the members of the sect that the businessman belonged to. It is interesting that similar behaviors still exist in modern society today where people are looked down upon because of religion, race, ethnicity, social class, and other stereotypes. In this case, there were two other members of the businessman's sector who had passed by the wounded man and realizing he was not one of them, just kept going.

How many times do we exhibit unkind behavior? After all, it is simple human decency to offer assistance when we come across those in need. The businessman was, however, of a different mindset. He indiscriminately showed the highest degree of humanity going above and beyond the normal course of action. In the spirit of human decency, he did what the others refused to do even though another human being was beaten and literally left to die in a ditch by the side of the road.

It might come to mind for some people that, oh, there will always be someone else to come to the rescue. That someone might be you. Maybe it was your turn to act, to show your humanity, to care for another human in need. Kindness should be an assumed responsibility by each of us. We never know what situation we could find ourselves in at any given time. Many of these circumstances have nothing to do with who we are or what we have. It's a fact. Life is like that. Things happen, unfortunate things can happen to anyone at any time.

Five Points of Kindness From a Stranger

1. He Stopped
2. He Attended to the Man's Wounds

3. He Carried Him
4. He Paid For the Man's Care
5. He Pledged to Stay Involved

Let's take a closer look at these five key points.

He Stopped.......

Personal responsibilities have not changed much from those days to the present. People were just as busy, trying to take care of business with the limited resources available during those times. For instance, traveling was so much harder than today. Transportation at that time was limited to horses or horse drawn carriages, if you could afford one. Donkeys and mules were the most common form of transportation, otherwise, you walked and that was definitely not much fun. Travel sometimes took several days depending on where one needed to go in order to conduct business or even for healthcare. So we can agree that there was never usually much time available on these trips.

Since we are familiar with how life in general was back then, I'm quite sure it makes it somewhat easier to appreciate the gravity of the circumstances. The kind man stopped when he saw the other in need of help. He put his business on hold; he paused for a very good cause. Our daily schedules are so intense these days, with so much happening in our lives. We hardly have enough time for ourselves no less make time for others. This I know makes it difficult at times for us to even notice others in need of help and assistance.

In addition, we must consider one's own personal safety. Once again, there's not much difference between then and now. Violent crimes existed as they do now and that is exactly what took place in this story. Let me make it extremely clear. I'm in no way telling you to take chances endangering yourself to find out if someone needs help. My aim is to encourage you to be aware of the need to show kindness and offer help when and where it's needed, if you are able to do so. However, I strongly recommend being cognizant of your personal safety. Having read this story, it has definitely brought on a keen awareness of both sides of the equation, performing a good deed and staying safe.

I am so encouraged every time I hear reports on the news about the good deeds and kindness of others, and it happens every day.

Remarkably enough, the kind hearted people are always referred to as "Good Samaritans,", and this story is exactly about the original account concerning this man from a place named Samaria. Not many of us know about this story in its' original form. I encourage you all to lend a hand whenever there's a need, lend a hand however you can, with whatever you can and be safe.

He Attended to the Man's Wounds

I spoke about the strict segregation laws and ordinances of that era in the Middle East, forbidden social interactions and bodily contact. Touching others from outside their sect, religion, class or race was totally forbidden. Again the good man indiscriminately touched and attended to the beaten man's injuries. This makes me wonder, that in the mind of the kind man, it was more important to help someone in need than to obey his religious laws. Did he on the other hand believe that his acts of kindness would be upheld by the teachings of his religion, would he be excused because he did a good deed? All religions teach us to be kind and do good deeds whenever and however we can.

He Carried the Wounded Man

The good Samaritan did not only stop and administer first aid with his limited resources, but also carried him to a place where he would receive proper medical attention. He was concerned about this man's welfare. More likely than not this man was a father, a husband, someone ordinary or someone important. Obviously it did not matter because to him it was necessary to do good and preserve life. This is what good does; good seeks out opportunities for the preservation of what is valuable to human existence. What a unique display of caring, even if one has to cross boundaries and go against the teachings of religion and culture.

He Paid For His Care

This becomes more noteworthy, more profound and enormously incredible under the circumstances. A total stranger did all this for someone he was forbidden to associate with, talk to, and touch. It is said that the two cultures had nothing to do with the other but he crossed the line because of the severity of the situation. We hear about similar acts of kindness quite often. Have you ever imagined yourself being on the receiving end?

Have you ever imagined yourself being on the giving end? I have been on both ends and it makes me wonder if some people are just naturally kind hearted. Were they on the receiving end of kindness and learned through that experience or maybe under the circumstances they had no choice or were compelled to get involved? Hopefully by now your mind is considering very deeply all you have read so far regarding this principle of showing kindness to someone who is in need. Be encouraged every time you hear reports of this nature. Assess yourself, and think about all the times you have passed by someone in need and you didn't offer assistance. Was it because you didn't have the resources? Were they not of your social class? Did it not matter? Were you too busy, or just couldn't be bothered? Whatever the case may be, always be reminded that you could one day be in need. The need may not be of a material or financial nature but it could be something more severe. We would under these circumstances wish someone would come to offer some assistance.

He Promised Future Payment

The good Samaritan showed so much humanity through his deeds and still went much further by taking on full financial responsibility for the robbed and wounded man. In promising to pay any additional cost incurred, he would have had to be think ing of checking in on the progress of his recovery on his way back. To me, that is going farther than above and beyond; that's going to the extreme. The question is, what drove him to do that? What drives another human being to risk their own life to save someone from a house on fire, or a burning car, how about raging flood waters, or other dangerous situations? We all have heard of, or may have witnessed things of this nature at one time or another. We call these people heroes, and rightly so. I know they did what was in their heart, the result of having a kind hearted nature or having learned what being kind is what drove them to action. They deserve more than just a medal or newsworthy notoriety. What is amazing about how they respond is when asked what prompted them into action, their answers always seem to be the same. It's usually "I saw someone in need, and I helped." I applaud all those who have sprung into action and showed kindness when it was most needed. You might say, "But I've never encountered anything like that." Be aware that opportunities to show kindness do not necessarily come in the form of severe difficulty. It is also about the little things you can do for someone, simple things that a lot of people walk away from.

Things like:

- Helping an older person up or down the stairs

- Helping a mother with a stroller and her kids get through a door

- Taking the time to give directions to some who's not sure how to get to a certain place

- Allowing a disabled person to go ahead of you

- Giving up your seat to a female or an elderly person.

- Offering to pay the extra amount for someone at the cash register who is short on cash

- Checking in on a neighbor you haven't seen in a while

These are just a few ways kindness can be shown to anyone. It does not take much to be kind. You will feel a lot better for taking just a few moments of your valuable time to help someone who could use a hand. Promise yourself that if you weren't actively offering help before, make that promise to start today. Get involved with an organization and volunteer in hospitals, clinics, youth groups or among other organizations and groups. Those are good places to start. You can also organize your own community help program. Mentor someone. There are kids and young people who are in need of tutoring. When you really think about it, there's a need for us to seriously involve ourselves in community affairs. When we build our communities, we are positively affecting our world. Better communities will result in a much better world.

Some people think that their contribution will most likely not make a big difference, but in doing nothing, one will never be able to find out whether or not that is true. I think of those whose legacy has lived throughout many decades and continue today, based on how much has been accomplished by one small act of kindness.

The Power of One

Most of us are familiar with the campaigning of Mahatma Gandhi for the freedom of his nation India, from British colonization. He was called to the Bar at age 22. He officially became a Lawyer. After practicing law for a number of years he became quite uncomfortable with British rule and the treatment of his countrymen. He was most certainly not the only one who had that concern. He was the one who took it upon himself to do something intentional and productive to positively change the situation. As a quick overview, he worked long and hard. He was beaten and imprisoned, ridiculed and excommunicated. He did not waiver in his mission to bring about change, the kind of change that brought freedom to the land he loved. In no way am I advocating that anyone endanger themselves for any cause no matter how noble it might be. My point is that this man saw a need and he committed himself to fight for change, for freedom, for dignity. He cared so much for the people, and the welfare of his fellow citizens was of great importance to him. Gandhi did what was in his heart and in the end his mission succeeded. The result was far reaching. His work has inspired many civil rights movements. Many civil rights leaders around the world have followed in his indelible foot prints, and have made significant impact to change the world. This is proof that a single individual can make a big difference in effecting change.

Another person whose acts of kindness changed the world is Mother Teresa. I doubt very much that most of us are unaware of her contribution to the sick, the poor, the orphaned and dying... This saintly woman dedicated her life to serve in areas and in ways that others would not venture. She cared for severely sick and diseased strangers for over forty five years and never regretted a single moment spent doing what some would not even remotely consider. Again we have additional proof that the effort and commitment of one person, starting with a single deed of offering help, can inspire the entire world. She founded The Missionaries Charity in India in 1950 and it continues today carrying on the tradition of providing humanitarian aid.

We could go on and on about the many individuals who have single handedly effected dramatic change, starting in a small corner of their community and how the impact has reach across the entire world. It would be a disservice not to recognize Dr. Martin Luther King Jr. whose unwavering determination, faith and tireless work brought freedom and equality to people from all ethnicities, economic and social backgrounds. This was one of modern day's most notable, and significant contributions to humanity.

To the many others who have done similar work and to those who are carrying on the legacy of these great spiritual leaders, we are truly indebted to you. We appreciate, applaud and are most grateful for your service. Never think that the little acts of kindness you offer are insignificant. It might very well be the starting point of something beyond your wildest dreams.

Your story of how you Rebounded from your former struggles can serve as a platform to help others bring change to their own lives. Do the best you can and be grateful for the life you now enjoy.

Personal Notes:

Personal Notes:

Personal Notes:

Chapter 9
Who Do I Want to Be?

Who Do I Want to Be?

Hopefully this won't be such a tough question for any of you to answer especially having come such a long way and having accomplished so much. If, however, at this point you're still not sure , now is the perfect time to find the answer and move on to become that person.

The word "who" in this case defines you as a person, not your job tittle, your qualifications, your net worth or anything else that has nothing to do with the kind of person you are. I have no intention of trying to confuse you in any way, but it should be understood that what a person has in terms of material objects, education, or money does not define who they are.

I know people who are well educated. Some are wealthy yet their personality leaves a lot of be desired. They have been described as, horrible, mean, nasty and so forth, some adjectives I would not care to mention in this book.

I'd like to reference a few categories which may somehow help to define or bring you closer to an answer to the above question.

1. How would you describe yourself?

2. Are you happy with who you are?

3. What would you change about yourself?

Having been in management, I've conducted many interviews and have noticed the reactions of candidates when they are asked to describe themselves. The question is usually, "Tell me about yourself?" Quite frequently it appears as if the question came as a surprise, somewhat unexpected. Most people seem to pause for a while as if to try and figure out what to say. Some common responses for starters are: "Ah let's see, Ok...... Let me put it this way....... I'm an ....person."

Some people constantly talk about themselves going on for hours but still not saying who they are. One could easily conclude that some people don't know who they are or are incapable of being truthful about who they really are. It is important to keep in mind that only you really know yourself. You know yourself better than anyone else. Even if you find it somewhat difficult to explain to yourself or another person, let me be quite clear that I fully understand the difficulty. Therefore it should be of paramount importance to everyone to be knowledgeable of who they really are. Having that knowledge will then make it so much easier to cope with outside influences which can cause instability in your thought process, behaviors, and how you live your life. If for any reason there are uncertainties, I would encourage you to take some time to seriously think about it and see what you might learn. I promise you things you never realize, understand or have even thought about will come to light in surprising ways.

Quite often I've heard people say, "I never knew this about myself" or "You know, I had no idea I was capable of such behavior." On the other hand, I've also heard, "I know me and that's why I didn't say or do anything." Will anyone ever fully know who they are? I think that is debatable and will not attempt to venture into such an intricate and delicate topic at this time. So for the record, let start with seeing how much we can learn about ourselves, to assist with enhancing our lives to the fullest.

Are You Happy With Yourself?

Again, we are faced with another question, and I think this is so deeply personal to everyone in both their private and public experiences. Like many of you, I'm no expert on the subject, but it's not that hard to look at someone and be able to see that they are unhappy. How often have you said to someone, "Hey, are you ok?" You've done it because you saw behaviors which indicated to you that something was wrong. Let's not confuse being generally happy and being unhappy with yourself. The distinction between the two is that a person who is normally happy can become unhappy about things that are happening around him or her, e.g., the death of a relative, a friend going through a hardship. In such a situation that individual would not be described as an unhappy person because that is not how they usually are. That state of being is just temporary and you'll find that before long they're back to being their regular self.

In the other case, we are referring to someone who is just generally unhappy, always unpleasant, upset about one thing or another, hard to get along with. Life is simply dull and boring. This usually is the result of some underlying issue or issues which have not being addressed or are difficult to reconcile. We can all think of people we know and come in contact with quite often. They may be family members, friends, and most certainly someone at work with whom interaction is necessary. These are the people who are unhappy and need to address their issues.

How would you honestly respond to the question being posed? Being unhappy with yourself is not always such a bad thing. There are advantages and disadvantages. One can be unhappy about attitudes and habits they have, things they do, not wanting to do, things they don't do that they should do. We talked about the apparent difficulty of changing especially bad habits, a certain kind of mindset which is unproductive. Not quite accomplishing certain goals within or at a particular point in life will cause a person to be unhappy with themselves because there's that feeling of disappointment.

In assessing yourself under this umbrella, try to identify any issue that may be a contributor and use those simple practices put forth earlier in this book to help improve in those areas of deficiency. There are many who have achieved much and still are not happy with themselves. It seems to them that there is more to accomplish. A void exists within those lives, a void that drives them to constant dissatisfaction and unhappiness. This of course is quite serious and should be dealt with on a professional level. I would strongly recommend seeking professional help.

On the other hand, being unhappy or dissatisfied with oneself can be advantageous in the sense that it prompts one into action to correct the situation. To many people it comes as a wakeup call. I know and have heard of several cases where people have kicked addictions and bad habits and have almost miraculously transformed their lives. They became totally unhappy about being unhappy. It's like enough is enough. They made the decision not to stay victims to the unpleasantness in their lives. They made the move; they Rebounded.

Where Are You Now?

What would you change about yourself?

All things considered, does it really matter? To whom does it matter, and why?

Yes...it does matter.....it should most certainly matter to you. The goal of this journey is to become a changed person, moving towards the life you've wanted. Here and now and going forward it must be about continuing to build on what you have already built, improving on the changes you have made and maintaining the momentum.

No one likes to lose, and it fascinates me to see a losing team, fighting to gain points even at 10 seconds or fewer to the end of the game. The mindset is....it's not quite over yet; we will play hard until the final buzzer goes off. When interviewed at the end of the game, the winners bask in the glory of victory; they celebrate; the team and fans are on top of the world. Honorable losers will recap and refer to all those missed opportunities and acknowledge the mistakes that were made. Being honest about their performance, they pledge to do things differently next time.

It makes a difference when you win at something. There's that feeling that is almost an indescribable feeling that only winners understand and appreciate. Of all the several ways to score at the hoop, I'm most impressed by a point gained from a Rebound... There's something special about making a comeback. A team or a player is down at a certain point in the game and then you look up and the score changes, the team, the player is up and eventually wins. Then the talk is about the big come back.

What would you change about you, to keep you moving forward, to keep you contented, successful and happy, and to keep being the best you can be? The answer lies within you; you decide what its worth to you, so yes it really does matter and it should matter to you. Anything in your life or about you that bugs you and makes you itch and uncomfortable, should be the thing or things you should want to change. There's no point in achieving much but still being unhappy.

In bringing this chapter to a close, let's take some time to make an assessment of yourself by identifying a few particular categories of people. Personalities, beliefs, customs, and attitudes are good indicators of who people really are.

The Diminishers

These are those who will put a damper on anything in terms of ones self- improvement, plans, ambition, success and things of that nature. They in some cases may even apply such negativities to themselves. It's not uncommon that they possess an innate habit of devaluing anyone's accomplishments. Not very much in their opinion is worthy of due recognition. This type of person will discourage enthusiasm and will stifle ambitions. They will tell you, that you can't, that it's out of your reach, you don't have what it takes, that you're aiming too high. Do you know anyone like that? Have you been unfortunate enough to live among or work alongside people who are unable to think otherwise?

I had a Boss years ago who laughed when I told him that I wanted a certain position that became vacant in the company. He literally laughed out loud, looked at me and said "you couldn't handle that." Imagine my surprise when I heard those words from someone who was supposed to be my mentor. Knowing who I am and what I'm made of, I told him "ok I'm going to show you that I can." Shortly thereafter the District Manager who knew me and clearly was of a different mindset came and offered me the position.

Don't let the naysayers influence your goals, plans or ambitions. Once you identify them, keep them away from you, especially now that you're on your way. You were somewhat stuck in the mud, you broke free, don't allow anyone or anything to "rain on your parade." This is now your party, your time to shine. It's your life, and you have a right to go after what you have always wanted. Once again be aware of bad influences. Anyone who does not have your best interest at heart should not be allowed in your circle.

The Illuminators

Your social and personal environment should consist of those with a positive mindset, the ones who believe that the possibilities are endless, people who see the good in you, and want you to succeed, and they believe in you. Some may not know for sure but they want the best for you and are aware that positive reinforcement can make a world of difference. They are the ones who place value on potential and intention. They will offer encouragement and cheer you on. Illuminators always look for and see the good in others. These are the kinds of associates you need. Everyone will need guidance at some time or another, so choose to be guided by people who will shine a light to help you navigate through the darkness, and help you through the difficulties. You can choose to be an illuminator in your own life and also in the lives of others; pledge to do for others, what you would want someone to do for you.

The Creators

How well do you think you would score in this category? Do you like the idea of building a strong foundation for the present and the future? Do you wake up with good ideas that can be put into action for the benefit of yourself and for others? I see simple gadgets almost every day that make certain chores so much easier, and I think "wow" this is such a great idea. This is really smart, and I wonder, did the inventor come up with the idea to create this. It's possible that some people are smart enough to figure things out and create. I also know that others will think long and work hard to find ways to create simple gadgets and highly technical mechanisms for just about every purpose. Again, the possibilities are endless and I tip my hat to all those who have put their ideas to work and have provided such conveniences to make life easier. In the same manner, never discard your idea or ideas if you believe there is an opportunity that it or they could be beneficial. Test those ideas in the appropriate ways; talk to people who will be able to steer you in the right direction. You can also just run with those ideas. You never know how they could materialize. All inventions simple or highly technical, started with an idea.

Hopefully you will be encouraged and stimulated by what you have read and learned, Hopefully you're in a much better position to determine who you really want to be. I also trust that you are definitely more self-assured and fully confident in knowing who you are.

The Innovators

"Innovation" is the introduction of something new or an improvement on an already existing, idea, product, or the way something is being done. Quite similar to invention and creativity, the difference however, is that innovation goes a step further and is an improvement on what is already in existence.

We have been focusing on self- improvement, self-renewal and Rebounding on the road to realizing one's full potential. The motivation then should be based on the idea that the sky is the limit and most definitely that the possibilities are endless. While this is not a tutorial on the subject, I find it necessary to mention a few examples just to get you motivated to see things and think of things from this point of view.

There are examples all around us. Most commonly, one electronic device that was designed solely for instant, long distance communication was "the telephone." For people like myself of a certain age group it is interesting to recall what this piece of technology was like in the early years of its invention compared to the transition of today's portable cell phones. If you were born around the last two and a half decades, you will agree that this is a perfect example of what innovation is all about. There's hardly anything that these new and improved "vital to life" pieces of technology cannot do or be used for. Every day technology advances to heights that are mind blowing. The telephone is just one.

So much is inside of each one of us that has been dormant, unknown, never thought of, or even imagined. It's your turn, your move, the ball is in your hands. Go for it, aim high and shoot straight. If you miss the hoop, go after that ball grab hold of it and try again. Make the decision about who you want to be, with determination, patience, dedication, commitment and the will to succeed. Become an Innovator. Become who you want to be.

Personal Notes:

Personal Notes:

Chapter 10
The Bottom Line

One of the most common phrases used today is, "The Bottom Line." It is used to pronounce finality, the bare facts, and the conclusion. It says, "It is what it is." We'll look at "the bottom line" as it relates to the contents of this book and your journey from where you were to where you are today.

The young CFO of one company I worked for used this phrase every day and in every conversation with everyone he had to deal with. It didn't matter who or what the subject of discussion was, including small talk. Every time I listened to him, I would always anticipate hearing those words and after a while it became predictable at what point in his partial monologue they would be said. Being the CFO, his primary responsibility was the financial well-being of the company and of course he would constantly be monitoring anything that would negatively affect the company's bottom line. Staff would be counseled and reprimanded if their conduct at any time even remotely threatened the financial health of the company.

In wrapping up this book we will recap in a step by step manner the best practices and suggestions which helped you to make that first step out of the situation you were in. I am fully aware that not all who have read the complete content of <u>Rebound</u> will reach their personal goal. There will be some who will, and are currently enjoying the result of the hard work, effort, sacrifices, dedication and determination it took to have rebounded to a life of satisfaction and fulfillment. Congratulations to you, you did an amazing job. Continue to enjoy and move forward, but please don't forget to lend a hand to someone. Remember, there are always a number of opportunities waiting.

We continue to root for those who are still in the process. Hang in there; as a matter of fact I'll say stand your ground and fight hard. Continue to stick with the plan, practice, practice, practice..... keep doing it until you get it. With very limited resources in 1878 Thomas Edison started his experiment with the goal of inventing the light bulb. He never gave up when it appeared impossible. He avoided the diminishers, those who said he was crazy when his early experiments failed several times. He kept at it because in his mind he knew that there was that possibility for success. Today others have improved on that technology teaching us that with a will and determination no task is impossible.

On March 7, 1876, Alexander Graham Bell successfully received a patent for the telephone and secured the rights to the invention. These and many other inventions and inventors are commonly known to us. We are currently enjoying the benefits of what was just a thought by some positive thinking individuals who decided not to give up on their dreams. The same can become reality for you in your quest for change, for new and better experiences. I personally love this word CHANGE, this concept, a desired goal to do something different, entering into a new way of living. It's all about renewal, making a comeback or starting out for the first time after realizing that there is a better way. Candles are not used solely for the purpose of illumination as before. The light bulb was invented and bought a new and better form of illumination. The possibilities are endless in your own personal situation.

Be the architect for your own transformation. Design what you want to see and how you want it to be. Only you know you in the most intimate way; only you know really know for sure what your deepest desires are. From the beginning, I have encouraged you to seek help from reputable sources if you believe you're unable to do it all by yourself. Seek advice from people who are equipped to help. Pattern someone who has their life together and is moving ahead or has already arrived. Be the builder of your own life. Use sound advice as the foundation, use good principles, the knowledge you've gained, encouragement you've gotten from honorable individuals. Discipline yourself to be consistent and if necessary, repeat it until it becomes second nature. These are your building blocks to a renewed life.

For those of you who haven't started or are still wondering about taking that first step, my advice to you, is to make the move, give it a shot. After all, what have you got to lose? Start with baby steps. Start seeing yourself better off than you currently are. You are at the starting point. You recognized the need for change and you have the desire. That's a great place to be. If your issue is low self- esteem, first realize that you are just as good as the person you wish you could be like. Train your mind to think that way, and say it to yourself repeatedly until you believe it. If you fall off track, get up and do it again and again until it becomes a habit.

Work on the areas where you are most vulnerable. Identify areas of opportunities, (some may call them weaknesses). Know that you're much stronger than you believe you are. It's there inside waiting to be awakened. Learn to force the negative thoughts that come to your mind. Don't let them take over, and begin to believe in yourself as being capable of change.

We talked about changing your environment. At times it may become necessary to actually change your physical environment. Sometimes you may also have to change your social environment. Surrounding yourself with positive, motivated people will prove to be a game changer. Plants will flourish in the right physical environment. I like to watch deer and their feeding pattern. I used to wonder why they're always on the sides of the road or in my front yard. As a practicing gardener, I was constantly annoyed with these animals. Then it dawned on me. They go where there are better plants to feed on. Even though they live in the very wooded area of the forest, they venture out to an environment where they can be properly fed. I learned how to securely fence my garden to keep them out.

Gravitate to whatever brings about and enhances positive change in your personal life. It's the only one you have and the only one you'll ever have. Don't waste time because of fear, or because they told you that you'll never be better off than you are. Prove to yourself first that you're worthwhile. You possess more than you can imagine, don't worry about what others think. Remember the young man who was born without limbs and all that he was able to accomplish through sheer determination and self-sacrifice. He kept trying over and over until he was able to maneuver his way up and down several flights of stairs with ease. In his own words one thing that carried him through was that he made it his mission to fight negative thoughts and told himself that he can achieve his goals.

Nothing is impossible if you put your mind to it and do what is necessary. A lot can be realized through simple, practical means. I have a deep interest in music and musicians, I'm always curious about how they mastered their instruments so skillfully. When listening to their story, the common thread is the countless hours of practice it took to perfect the art of playing so masterfully. They tried and tried and even when they became discouraged and it seemed futile, they continued because mastery was what they were after.

So just as the old man that played his violin on the sidewalk told the young aspiring musician, "you get to Carnegie Hall by practice... Practice, Practice, Practice, don't be afraid to make mistakes." If you do, start over. You're guaranteed to learn something very valuable. If you fumble the ball, don't despair; go after it even when it's in the hands of your opponent. Chase after it because the goal is to retrieve it and make a run for the end zone.

The bottom line here is that the responsibility to succeed is yours. You are in charge of your destiny, and there are resources available for you to Rebound to a renewed life no matter how bad your situation appears to be. If you change your way of thinking from the negative to the positive, accompanied by the right attitude and action, you will succeed. Regardless of why you found yourself at a disadvantage and you're not happy with the way things are, in order for you to realize the satisfaction you want, you must make that move. Believe in your self-worth but most importantly, believe in something bigger and stronger than you.

Let's Recap:

If you were asked, what is your biggest take away from reading this book, what would it be?

Have you any idea what your greatest strength, strengths is, are?

What is holding you back?

Why do you believe whatever it is has such a hold on you?

If you are still undecided, that is understandable. We all don't have the same capabilities.

We do not all possess the same ability to recover at the same pace. While some are more apt to jump into action others will hesitate for a while before moving ahead. Hopefully none of you will procrastinate to the point of never taking that first step. I will strongly emphasize that nothing will happen. Change will not begin until that first step is taken. Remember if necessary, take baby steps to start doing the most important thing you'll ever do in your life.

You did the right thing by picking up this book. Great job! Your journey has begun. Don't waste your life simply because you did not believe there was a way out. There is no problem without a solution. Sometimes the solution is simple and of course sometimes it is a bit more difficult, but there is a solution.

You can realize the change you've been wanting. You can smile again, and step out into the world as a brand new person. Arm yourself with what you've read, absorb it, allow it to sink deep inside you and become you. Trample on your fears, crush doubtful thoughts, say the words out loud if you have to.

I CAN DO

I CAN MOVE FORWARD

I CAN WIN

I'M NOT AFRAID ANYMORE

SUCCESS IS MINE

I WILL FIGHT HARD, NO MATTER HOW LONG IT TAKES

In my current capacity, I see many good people who are trapped, seemingly helpless, people who have given up on life. Their existence is summed up in "I'll take what comes to me, whatever happens." It brings such sadness; it makes me wish that I could wave a wand and open their eyes to the truth. I want to tell them, "hey there is a better way, a better way to live but it's only possible when you acknowledge your situation, admit to yourself, the truth, the truth being that you want change."

Unfortunately certain elements in our society have conditioned the minds of the weak and underprivileged to think and feel that way. Sadly, too many people believe this. They should be taught to think for themselves. When it comes to your life, the issues that weigh you down, treat it, or them as a priority. You my friend have the right to be a success, making a tangible and positive contribution to the community, and to the world to make things better for the children who will come and be here after we're gone. How disturbing it is to see babies living in less than acceptable conditions, less than what can be considered healthy. Parents aren't setting the right example so these little ones grow up not knowing that life doesn't have to be that way.

If you are a parent struggling with issues that affect your ability to set the right example for your children, realize that now you have the tools to start making a change. Don't let those little ones get lost in the same way you were. Use these valuable resources to create a new way of thinking to build a better life for you and your children. They are so precious and should be valued above all. They are yours, a gift, they are yours to love and care for.

So, what's your bottom line?

- The bottom line is, unless you step up and step out, change won't be a reality.

- The bottom line is, all things are possible

- The bottom line is, there are no problems without a solution The bottom line is, change that mindset

- The bottom line is, be determined, practice, be repetitive

- The bottom line is, be consistent, believe in your abilities, find your inner strengths

Personal Notes:

Personal Notes:

Chapter 11
Looking Back

Let's take a look at some of the people and situations we examined throughout our reading. Before we go on, remember that repetition is vital in perfecting new habits. I also know that taking a second look at anything always allows one to discover so much more than what was seen or noted from just a first look. Keeping your goals at the forefront of your mind is a must when it comes to maintaining your focus. You need positive reinforcement to be assured that your efforts make sense and that you're moving in the right direction. Be purposeful and resolute, especially because there is a real and important reason for starting this life saving adventure.

I think of Steve, the young man from the Islands who came to the United States in search of a better life. Sure, you remember him, the one who slept on the subway and went to night school. Quite a handsome, strong, but very quiet man. It was somewhat uncomfortable to be around Steve when we first met and became friends, because he hardly spoke. He was not shy, just quiet but when he spoke, you were compelled to listen. I never asked him what led to the hardship that made him homeless but he told me somethings about his life before he came here and it was quite interesting. I believe that he'd always wanted to live here in the U S. to enjoy the kind of life he envisioned for himself. For him it was an important goal and the only focus he had. He decided to take that first step and put his thoughts into action.

Steve was an accomplished musician, in fact he taught me a few things of real value about playing the guitar and also about singing, and boy could he hold a harmony. When I met Steve, he had already rebuilt his life and was doing very well. He had a great job on Wall Street, a beautiful home and a wonderful wife, so it was not easy to imagine what he later explained. He experienced some tough situations to get to where he was, accomplished and living a fulfilled life. Most people would not have done what he did to achieve a goal. Again, my point is, anything is possible if you put your mind to it. You might say, well I certainly wouldn't do what he did. Then find another way, a means by which you can bring about change in your life. Whatever and however you choose to do it, will require most, if not all of the same principles and determination suggested throughout this book.

I rewatched the videos of the two young men I came across on YouTube. The one man without arms, who played the guitar with his toes, is astounding. I still can't rationalize it; it's not only the toes doing what fingers should do but also I know how difficult a task that is. It must have taken a strong sense of determination and a strong mindset to persevere. "He blew that out of the water" as is commonly said. What then could be stopping you from blowing the things that restrict you out of the water? Change the mindset, see only possibilities, be single minded, and make that move. Who would have thought that a body without "limbs" designed for movement, could ever move up and down a stairway, a body with just a head, and a strong mind. The mind is the real you; the mind is where one's self is fashioned. That is where it starts, is maintained and executed. You are the only one who can make it happen. You are in command of what the outcome will be. The young man without limbs blew his disabilities out of the proverbial water. He danced, without limbs. He was a member of the dance group at his school. Watching that video was an experience I never thought I would witness and it is still mind blowing every time I think of it. It all happens in the mind, your thoughts can make you, they can release and unleash your full potential. Thoughts can break down barriers you felt were unbreakable. Good and positive thoughts will allow you to grow wings so you can fly higher than you ever imagined. Give it a try and you'll see results beyond expectations.

On the other hand, thoughts can keep you in bondage, and at a gross disadvantage. The negative thoughts will nail you to a cross. They tell you, no... that's not possible, it won't happen for you, you're not good enough. Harness the power of your negativity and turn it around for good, be your boss. Change your way of thinking; it's guaranteed to change you, your life, and your world.

For Michael, things could have been very different if he had made some adjustments to his way of thinking There is nothing wrong with failing at times as long as you are prepared to learn, change the way you play the game, do it over and over again until you get it right. A positive attitude will transport you to unimaginable heights, you will break down barriers and walk out of the rubble into newness. Take constructive criticism, seek sound advice, be mentored, and ask for direction and clarification of what is not understood or easily understood. Michael could have realized his goals and been better off than he is today, instead of living with regrets and still placing the blame on others. Never blame others for what you think are the reasons for your failures. It is your responsibility, your life, so take charge of it in the best possible way.

I will remind you, and I feel no shame in saying that I have been where most of you are, felt what most of you are feeling, and had similar thoughts of defeat. I was blinded to the truth as much as anyone. I could not see a way out, was afraid, terrified at times. I wondered what was happening and why? I don't deserve this, life is mean and unfair, Why? Hitting bottom was what woke me up. It opened my eyes and forced me to take that first move and eliminated procrastination from my life. It wasn't easily done, but all the hard work and effort put towards taking control, paid off and it paid off really well.

Jason had the best family life anyone could want but nobody told him he would have unfortunate experiences. The man was almost perfect; he did everything right, he was loved by his parents and had nothing to worry about. But as simple as what he went through sounds, it was real. The ordeal nearly destroyed him but he found a way to bring himself back to who he really was and changed the course of what appeared to be hopelessness into the fulfillment of his dreams. He found love and built his family and progressed in his career. His decision not to let the negative elements invade his mind and stay there was the best thing he ever did.

You may have it all, but feel there is something missing or seriously wrong in your life, something you seem unable to shake. Look back at the folks you read about and what they achieved. I said before that it doesn't matter how much help you receive professionally. If you don't put that advice into practice, nothing will change. Only look back to measure your progress and use that measurement to plan your next step further and further away from the past.

The only one stopping you is you. In most oppressive situations we are our worst enemy. We stand in our own way and prevent ourselves from moving forward. Just think about it. Unwillingness, procrastination and fear are some of the biggest barriers we face, but as difficult as they appear, I encourage you to make that move. Take a real stand and fight for your life, success is just beyond those so called barriers.

A confident man as David Trotter was, he was badly shaken and lost his composure once he realized he was late for the biggest presentation of his life. As shaken and worn out as he felt, he walked into Dayton Enterprises knowing it was late and that there was a possibility he wouldn't get a chance to be seen, but he went anyway. He could have given up, and he almost did. He could have walked away but he didn't. Always remember, nothing is as bad as it appears. Be bold! After taking time to regain his composure, he made quite a masterful presentation which landed him the biggest contract of his business. Don't tell me it can't be done, don't stop for anything when going after your goals. Don't allow anyone or anything to stand in the way of your progress. Good things never come easily, especially when you're starting out or restarting, but be determined.

The teenage shepherd boy, young David, fought a lion to protect what was in his care, the thing which was given to him as a responsibility. He put his life on the line. The diminishers tried to discourage him when he said he could defeat the giant that intended to destroy his people. Yes, they tried several times. The more they tried, the more he was encouraged and determined to do what was in his heart. He was persistent, he was motivated, he was focused and he won in the end. The diminishers were put to shame. He proved that he was capable. His victory saved an entire nation. The power of one. Are you ready to face your Lion? Are you ready to conquer the Giant in your life?

Irina didn't dwell on the fact that through no fault of her own, her budding career was interrupted and she could no longer perform competitively. She could no longer share her talent with the world but even after years of heartache and a feeling of hopelessness, she came to the realization that life doesn't have to be miserable. She did what was necessary. She did what was the only thing to do under the circumstances. "Life can be worthwhile again. I can touch lives again. I can help to make the lives of little girls happy", she thought. That's when she sprang into action. It all starts with a thought, a good thought. Then you act on it and are persistent. She did it; her dreams became reality, even though they were somewhat different from her original dream. She found fulfillment in making a valuable contribution to the lives of those who otherwise probably would not have been able to become what they themselves dreamed of. Stick to the plan and stay on course.

Will made up his mind not to let his life be guided by his traumatic childhood experiences. Instead of taking out his frustration on society or other people who were not at fault, he took a job early in life. He learned responsibility. He realized that no one would do it for him. It was his choice, success or failure? Which was it going to be? He learned how to make sure that he would not be blamed by his children for being the reason for their unhappy childhood. After finding his inner strength and his true potential, there was no stopping him. He kept on going. He used to be an employee of the Government, now he supplies the Government with necessary services.

I'm feeling excitement for all of you at this very moment and each time I read and re-read this book. I'm also very hopeful that change has come to you as an individual. Yes I'm extremely encouraged and full of anticipation knowing that many of you will smile again, laugh again, and feel free again. You are now empowered; you now know that the controls are in your hands. Hold on tight and steer in the right direction!

There is a whole new world out there to be experienced compared to the old horrible one you've known, believing there's nothing else but gloom. Stand your ground. Don't just hang in there. There is no stability when you're hanging. In order to succeed, you need to be firm and resolute. Be single minded. As it is said, put on blinders if necessary to guard against distractions, tune out the noise, the voices that tell you otherwise. In other words, maintain those good habits you've developed, be on guard that you don't slip back into previous behaviors which aren't helpful to your new self. Continue spending time on self-structuring, working on yourself, taking care of your body, your mind, your appearance, how you present yourself.

Stay active; don't allow too much time for not doing anything constructive, but do not forget to stop and smell the roses. Learn to relax, do not sweat the small stuff, and avoid adding stress to your life. Worrying about things doesn't change their existence or their outcome. Endeavor to find solutions, and take it as an opportunity to think broadly and be bold. Don't have a lotto mentality. Don't depend on luck or wait for a miracle, note that nothing comes to you for free; you have to go after it. When you do, go with faith, and expect positive results. Your efforts will bring astounding returns and you'll be better off.

It remains extremely important to seek help from good sources, so we have added some valuable resources that you will find helpful, both to get started and also to maintain your focus. Let me also remind you that you must be careful and aware of your association with others. Again, surround yourself with those who will honestly cheer you on to success. I find that there is a large number of genuinely helpful and kind hearted individuals who are always ready and willing to help. Stop at nothing to find these individuals and take advantage of all that is available to assist you on your journey. This is your life, the most precious thing you have and will ever have. Make the most of it, make the best of it, and in turn help someone else to Rebound.

A Personal Note

Let me say that all that I have written in order to encourage you to start your journey to rebound are best practices I've used in my own life. My journey may not have been as difficult as some simply because I realized at an early stage that there was an inevitable need to effect the change necessary for my moving ahead. Fortunately, after doing a thorough self-examination over quite some time, I made the decision to step up and step out into the unknown. I used all the best practices suggested and repeated them until they became a part of me. Let me say that it wasn't all that easy, but I eventually grasped the know-how, step by step, and sometimes using baby steps. I told myself the same things I'm telling you, day after day until they became a habit. Today I'm in control of the things that controlled me. My life is different, better, stress free. I'm so glad I made it a priority.

My friends, it is time to wake up, and do great things; discover who you really are, and start to shine. See yourself as fully capable; see yourself always as a winner. Regardless of what your beginnings were, whether you had the traditional home life with mom and dad present and involved. Whether you only had a mom who was caring and did her best, or one who did not. Did you grow up in a dysfunctional family, were you adopted, were you abandoned? You can't go back and fix the past. Don't keep dwelling on the past, the past that you try to forget but just can't seem to kick the persistent unpleasant memories. It haunts you day and night. You stay in that place where you wish things were different. Well, they are. You have to leave that behind and push forward. The here and now is what you have; change it now before it's too late. Remember, time waits for no one, so don't be left behind.

Encouraging You

Throughout this book, my goal has been to keep on cheering you on as long as you move towards what you've been searching for. I continue to encourage you, and hope that you'll stay encouraged. Stay hopeful but don't just depend on hope. To realize your goal or goals, action is of vital importance, and these actions must be repetitive. My friends, be encouraged and stay encouraged. Go after the ball if you lose it. Fight and take the shot. Head for the end zone with everything you've got and do that dance when you touch down.

My Best Wishes to You All!

Thank you for taking the time to read this book!

May God Bless You, May You Bless Others.

REBOUND

Personal Notes:

Personal Notes:

Will I Seek Help?
Refer to Chapter 3

As mentioned in Chapter 3, talk to those you know who are capable and will have your interest at heart. Make sure the ones you consult are persons who have their lives together and are able to offer sound advice.

Here, make a list of people/agencies to consult with when you need help and/or sound advice:

Trusted Friend:

Family members:

Therapists:

Doctors:

Below, please find additional resources…

You're on your way, on the move, on a life-saving mission…

Resources

Below is a list of resources, please note that the contact information may have changed since the publication of the book

Mental Health Providers/Resources:

- Betterhelp.com
- Brightside.com
- Brightspacecoaching.com
- Cerebral.com
- Management.org
- Online-therapy.com
- Psychology Today
- Regain.us
- Talkiatry.com
- Teencounseling.com
- Try.talkspace.com

Resources

Spiritual Resources:

- Faithful Counseling-Betterhelp.com
- Family
- Faith in my beliefs and the process
- Mediation
- Outdoor Activities
- Prayer
- Running
- Social Groups
- Writing

Mentoring Plan
Refer to Chapter 5

Adopt a Mentor Strategy
Someone or Something to look up to

Mentoring is individualized as it focuses on the individual

Mentoring is individualized, and the ability to push someone's thinking

Characteristics of a good mentoring relationship:

- Trust
- Mentoring should be tailored to individualized needs

Effective Strategies to Build Capacity Through Mentoring

Mentoring creates an opportunity to broaden perspectives, examine assumptions, and share expertise to support adult development.

Mentoring can take many forms, such as teaming or pairing up with someone or a group who may have or can offer more knowledge about a particular subject or concept to improve and deepen your overall knowledge, interest, growth, and/or development.

Growth in adulthood should be consistent especially when an individual is willing to become a sponge. When he or she comes to the realization that I can learn something new today and I can go further than yesterday, you are on the right path.

Growth happens when you have a passion for a subject/topic and want to learn more. Growth happens when there is a challenge and/or passion to know something or answer a burning question. For example, talk about my research question, which has been a thorn in my side for years- What is the relationship between school services and the rate of suspensions in small urban New York City public schools? Growth also happens when you are in an environment that challenges your thinking and in life experiences

Challenges to Find a Mentor

Connecting and networking with people in the field can be a challenge as well as time consuming requiring financial resources. Some people may not be at arm's reach, which may require one to go through or jump a few hurdles to get there

Mentors should provide the following:

Good and effective feedback

Increase confidence

Encouragement

Opportunities to discuss

Time to meet

Trust

Action Plan

Goal _____

Objective _____

WHAT **Objective**	
HOW *Major Tasks/Activities*	
WHEN *Beginning Date*	
SUPPORTS NEEDED *Resources*	
INDICATORS OF SUCCESS	
ACCOUNTABILITY *Person(s) Responsible*	

Action Plan

Goal _____

Objective _____

WHAT **Objective**	
HOW *Major Tasks/Activities*	
WHEN *Beginning Date*	
SUPPORTS NEEDED *Resources*	
INDICATORS OF SUCCESS	
ACCOUNTABILITY *Person(s) Responsible*	

Works Cited

National Center for Health Statistics. (2003, April). Retrieved from cdc.gov

Pew Research Center. (2019, December 12). Retrieved from www.pewresearch.org

(2021). Retrieved from Congressional Coalition on Adoption Institute.

(2022, June 15). Retrieved from Psychologytoday.com: www.psychologytoday.com

(2024, February 21). Retrieved from mentorloop.com: https://mentorloop.com

We all have the ability to change, to make better choices, and to become valuable members of our community.

About the Author

Linval R. Morris brings a wealth of knowledge and experience to this project that is very dear and of great concern to him. He has been involved in church and community outreach from a very young age by organizing and leading study groups, public speaking, and interactive activities geared toward individual self-advancement.

After high school and college, he traveled extensively throughout Europe and several Caribbean islands. In his travels, he always seemed to have people from all walks of life share their personal concerns with him. This sparked a strong interest and concern for those people and others who struggle with finding ways to move themselves toward success and achieving their personal goals.

All the jobs he's held have one thing in common and that is constant interaction with people through Management, Consulting, Community Based Social Services, and Business Ownership.

His hope for the future is to officially establish and organization to further reach those in need of help, encouragement, and training to change their circumstances and better their lives.

He believes that no one should feel left out, helpless, and lack resources to improve not only their lives but also the community as a whole.

His expectation is that this book will serve as a source of encouragement and inspiration to all who will take the time to read it.

Please follow Rebound on:
LinkedIn
Instagram
Facebook

www.ingramcontent.com/pod-product-compliance
Lightning Source LLC
LaVergne TN
LVHW051049080426
835508LV00019B/1783